Reformation Questions,
Reformation Answers

Also by Donald K. McKim

The Church: Its Early Life
The Authority and Interpretation of the Bible:
    An Historical Approach (with Jack B. Rogers)
The Authoritative Word: Essays on the Nature of Scripture (editor)
Readings in Calvin's Theology (editor)
What Christians Believe about the Bible
A Guide to Contemporary Hermeneutics:
    Major Trends in Biblical Interpretation (editor)
How Karl Barth Changed My Mind (editor)
Ramism in William Perkins' Theology
Theological Turning Points: Major Issues in Christian Thought
Major Themes in the Reformed Tradition (editor)
Encyclopedia of the Reformed Faith (editor)
Kerygma: The Bible and Theology (4 volumes)
The Bible in Theology and Preaching
Westminster Dictionary of Theological Terms
God Never Forgets: Faith, Hope, and Alzheimer's Disease (editor)
Historical Handbook of Major Biblical Interpreters (editor)
Historical Dictionary of Reformed Churches
    (with Robert Benedetto and Darrell L. Guder)
Calvin's Institutes: *Abridged Edition* (editor)
Introducing the Reformed Faith: Biblical Revelation,
    Christian Tradition, Contemporary Significance
The Westminster Handbook to Reformed Theology (editor)
The Cambridge Companion to Martin Luther (editor)
Presbyterian Beliefs: A Brief Introduction
Presbyterian Questions, Presbyterian Answers
The Cambridge Companion to John Calvin (editor)
Calvin and the Bible (editor)
Historical Dictionary of Reformed Churches, 2nd ed.
    (with Robert Benedetto)
Dictionary of Major Biblical Interpreters (editor)
Ever a Vision: A Brief History of Pittsburgh Theological Seminary, 1959–2009
More Presbyterian Questions, More Presbyterian Answers
A "Down and Dirty" Guide to Theology
Living into Lent
Coffee with Calvin: Daily Devotions
The Westminster Dictionary of Theological Terms, rev. and exp.
Presbyterian Faith That Lives Today
John Calvin: A Companion to His Life and Theology
Moments with Martin Luther: 95 Daily Devotions

Reformation Questions, Reformation Answers

 Key Events, People, and Issues

Donald K. McKim

 WESTMINSTER
JOHN KNOX PRESS
LOUISVILLE · KENTUCKY

© 2017 Donald K. McKim

First edition
Published by Westminster John Knox Press
Louisville, Kentucky

17 18 19 20 21 22 23 24 25 26—10 9 8 7 6 5 4 3 2 1

Book design by Sharon Adams and Allison Taylor
Cover design by Allison Taylor

Library of Congress Cataloging-in-Publication Data
Names: McKim, Donald K., author.
Title: Reformation questions, Reformation answers : 95 key events, people, and issues
  / Donald K. McKim.
Description: Louisville, KY : Westminster John Knox Press, 2017.
Identifiers: LCCN 2016032964 (print) | LCCN 2016034578 (ebook) | ISBN
  9780664260606 (pbk. : alk. paper) | ISBN 9781611647822 (ebook)
Subjects: LCSH: Reformation--Miscellanea.
Classification: LCC BR308 .M45 2017 (print) | LCC BR308 (ebook) | DDC
  270.6--dc23
LC record available at https://lccn.loc.gov/2016032964

Most Westminster John Knox Press books are available at special quantity discounts when purchased in bulk by corporations, organizations, and special-interest groups. For more information, please e-mail SpecialSales@wjkbooks.com.

Jack Hemingway McKim

*May he be blessed with the living faith
of the Protestant Reformers*

Contents

History

Theology

5. Theological Topics of Christian Faith   70

6. Dividing Issues among Protestants   87

x   Contents

Legacy

Preface

In 2017 millions of Christians throughout the world will celebrate or commemorate the 500th anniversary of the Protestant Reformation. This anniversary looks back to the actions of Martin Luther who published his Ninety-five Theses on October 31, 1517, an event commonly considered as the trigger of a reformation—and revolution!—that changed the face of Europe and the rest of the world.

The Protestant Reformation is one of the most studied events of the Western world. Scholars from various disciplines have written on the events of the period from the sixteenth to mid-seventeenth century, a range of time in which momentous events took place. These scholarly perspectives enhance our understandings of the issues and complexities of what transpired when challenges to the Roman Catholic Church changed the entire religious landscape.

This book cannot take the place of studying the Reformation through many lenses. It does not provide a full look at Reformation history, theology, or its legacy, the major focuses this book does have. A number of excellent resources on the Reformation are listed in the further reading section, their insights and information waiting to be discovered. I hope this book will spur study of these fine sources and many others.

Much more modestly, this book primarily provides a look at important aspects of Reformation history and theology through a series of questions and answers. This format presents capsulized snapshots to acquaint readers with backgrounds, leading persons, events, and developments of the history of the Reformation. More questions and answers look at the theology of the Reformation through various theological expressions associated with the period, theological topics of Christian faith that were important to the church and its reformers, as well as some dividing issues among Protestants that evoked contentious theological debates among the churches of the Reformation era. A final group of questions and answers relate to the legacy of the Reformation and the heritage the Reformation has established. A time line relates to the questions and answers, and the further reading section provides some next steps in Reformation study with vastly more context and detail than is provided here. Of course, abundant materials are also found on the Internet.

My hope is that this book will stimulate interest in the Protestant Reformation among students in various contexts as well as with church groups and church members. On many levels the Reformation period was vastly significant for political, social, cultural, religious, military, and theological reasons. This book provides a way to dip into some main historical and theological events and issues. It provides an overview of what was going on and why certain things were—and are—tremendously important.

My study of the Reformation has been of long-standing, through years as a pastor, seminary professor and dean, author, and editor for Westminster John Knox Press. Teachers and colleagues who have brought the Reformation alive for me have been treasured blessings. Those who have written works over the centuries to explore the era have provided a great service, for which we can be thankful.

My family always provides the love and support needed to write my books. I owe my wonderful wife, LindaJo, more than I can ever say; so I express my deepest love and gratitude to her. Our son Stephen and his wife, Caroline, and their daughters, Maddie and Annie, bless us so much. Our son Karl and his wife, Lauren, give us joys, and we treasure our times together.

This book is dedicated to the newest member of our family, Jack Hemingway McKim. Jack joins his sisters, Maddie and Annie, as LindaJo's and my beloved grandchildren. I wish Jack a blessed and joyful life in the service of God in Jesus Christ, the life Protestant Reformers sought for all persons.

I would also like to thank three splendid publishing professionals at Westminster John Knox Press whose help is deeply appreciated. David Dobson, Julie Tonini, and Daniel Braden are valued former colleagues and treasured friends.

For Reformation 2017 and beyond, I hope this book can serve as a small, introductory guide to what transpired during the Reformation period and what theological issues were considered of deep significance to those who sought reform of the Christian church. These were dedicated Christians who wanted to listen and understand God's word to the church, expressed in the Scriptures, and supremely in God's Son, Jesus Christ. By the power of the Holy Spirit, they believed God was at work in the world and in the church to guide Christian disciples into ways of obedience to Jesus Christ. God's Spirit continues to guide the church today, as we follow Jesus Christ and listen to God's word. We can learn from the sixteenth-century Reformers as we heed the call in the book of Isaiah: "Look to the rock from which you were hewn, and to the quarry from which you were dug" (Isa. 51:1).

Donald K. McKim
Germantown, Tennessee
September 2016

Time Line

1530	Diet of Augsburg and Augsburg Confession
1534	English Parliament passes legislation establishing the Church of England
1534	Luther's German Bible published
1535	End of Anabaptist rule in Münster
1536	John Calvin arrives in Geneva; first edition of *Institutes* published
1538	Calvin expelled from Geneva; ministers in Strasbourg
1539	"Great Bible" published in England and authorized for English churches
1540	Society of Jesus recognized by Roman Catholic Church
1541	Calvin returns to Geneva and continues his ministries
1541	Regensburg Colloquy
1542	Roman Inquisition established by Pope Paul III
1545	Council of Trent begins
1549	The *Book of Common Prayer* published for the Church of England
1549	*Consensus Tigurinus* (Zurich Agreement) between Calvin and Bullinger
1553	Mary Tudor becomes Queen; Protestant exiles leave England
1555	Peace of Augsburg
1556	Thomas Cranmer burned at the stake
1557	Index of Prohibited Books published under Pope Paul IV

1558	Elizabeth I becomes Queen of England
1559	Religious Settlement in England
1559	Final Latin edition of Calvin's *Institutes*
1560	Reformation in Scotland and Scots Confession published
1560	Geneva Bible published
1561	Colloquy at Poissy, France
1562	First War of Religion in France
1563	Council of Trent adjourns
1563	Thirty-nine Articles published for the Church of England
1563	Heidelberg Catechism published
1568	Bishops' Bible published in England
1572	St. Bartholomew's Day Massacre of Huguenots in France
1577	Formula of Concord adopted by Lutherans
1580	Lutherans adopt *Book of Concord*
1598	Edict of Nantes
1604	Hampton Court Conference authorizes new English translation of Bible
1610	Roman Catholic Douai-Rheims Bible published as English translation
1611	King James Bible published in England
1618	Thirty Years' War begins
1618	Synod of Dort begins in The Netherlands
1642	English Civil War begins

History

1

Backgrounds

1 What was the Reformation?

"Reformation" (Lat. *reformatio*) is a term for assorted religious reforms that took place throughout Europe in the sixteenth century. These varied in many ways, and some historians prefer to speak of "European Reformations" instead of a single "European Reformation." Yet there are bonds of connection among the diverse movements and shared, common characteristics. Together, the movements sought to reform the Western church in ways that went beyond previous movements both in what they advocated and the degree to which fundamental changes were enacted.

The "Protestant Reformation" was marked by a focus on Scripture as the primary theological authority for the church, rejecting the authority of the pope and the traditions of the Roman Catholic Church. The church (and society) was to be reformed on the basis of Scripture.

Additional theological emphases were developed by Protestant Reformers. Some prominent leaders were Martin Luther (1483–1546), Huldrych Zwingli (1484–1531), John Calvin (1509–1564), and Menno Simons (1496–1561). These theological convictions were far-reaching in their scope in critiquing traditional Roman Catholic theology, even as the Reformers differed on theological particulars among themselves.

The Reformation is often seen as embracing the period between the sixteenth century to the middle of the seventeenth century. A number of proposed changes in the church in this era had been prepared for in the two centuries preceding the sixteenth century. Traditionally, the Protestant Reformation is viewed to have begun with the publication of Luther's Ninety-five Theses in Wittenberg on October 31, 1517. But Luther's understandings had developed in years prior to this event itself, even as theological developments were occurring within different thinkers and Christian groups.

Various church movements and traditions emerged from these tumultuous times of church reform and religious change. The impact and legacy of the Reformation are with us today in significant ways. Those who lived in Europe in this period were conscious of changes occurring. They also faced personal choices about their understanding of the Christian faith and how their faith was to be lived. The Protestant Reformation provided ways of understanding Scripture and understanding the church, which offered new directions for Christian people.

2 What began the Reformation?

The Protestant Reformation in Germany is traditionally understood as beginning with Martin Luther's posting of his "Ninety-five Theses" on the church door of the castle church in Wittenberg, Germany, where Luther was a theology professor. The date was the eve of All Souls' Day, October 31, 1517. This set in action a chain of events that led to Luther's excommunication from the Roman Catholic Church, in which Luther was priest, and the development of Luther's theological viewpoints that began the Protestant movement.

Luther's Ninety-five Theses focused on the Roman Catholic practice of issuing indulgences. These certificates could be purchased from the church to reduce the penalties for sins being paid by relatives in purgatory as they were being painfully purified before entering heaven. Luther believed this practice was unbiblical.

Posting theses for academic debate was the common practice in university settings, and Luther sought to debate these theses with colleagues. Some scholars have doubted whether the actual posting of the theses took place. But, when the published theses were circulated by Luther's friends through German cities, a reaction far greater than Luther could have imagined began. The German Reformation was under way.

In Switzerland, Huldrych Zwingli was priest of the Great Cathedral in Zurich. In 1519, he began the revolutionary practice of preaching directly through the Gospel of Matthew, instead of following the Roman Catholic lectionary. Zwingli's preaching drew comparisons between the New Testament church and the church of his present day. In 1522, when Zwingli's preaching emboldened some to break the church's traditional fast of not eating meat during Lent—they ate sausages—Zwingli defended those who broke the fast and increased his calls for church reform. The Swiss Reformation was under way.

Zwingli worked to spread the reform throughout Switzerland and into other lands, each of which had their own experiences of the Reformation.

❸ How did the Reformation develop?

The Protestant Reformation had many facets and can be viewed from a number of angles. Historical dimensions provided the contexts in which important events occurred. Theological developments fueled the ongoing developments of various church bodies and political and social activities. Studies of the Reformation can focus on these various directions and enrich our understandings.

One broad outline of the religious activities of sixteenth-century Reformation developments includes the following:

(1) *Backgrounds* (1500–1520). During the late medieval period, there were various calls for reform of the Roman Catholic Church in its life, morals, and institutional forms. The humanist movement, and especially Desiderius Erasmus (c. 1466–1536), gave impetus to these reform initiatives.

(2) *Development* (1520–1530). Martin Luther's critiques of the Roman Catholic practice of indulgences (1517) led to the church's excommunication of Luther. Yet Luther's interpretations of Scripture and developing theology—especially the doctrine of justification by faith alone (see question 65)—were aided by access to

his thoughts through the growing printing industry. The work of Huldrych Zwingli in Zurich led to the growth of the Reformed theological tradition. Controversies over infant baptism led to the Anabaptist movement.

(3) *Expansion and response* (1530–1563). In England, the Protestant Reformation had two phases when rulers adopted the Protestant way. The first was when King Henry VIII established the English church (1534) and Protestantism was strengthened under Edward VI (1547–1553). The second was, after the reign of the Roman Catholic Queen Mary I (1553–1558), with the reign of Elizabeth I from 1558 onward. The political defeat of the Puritan movement meant the Church of England (later, Anglicanism) continued as the official Protestant faith. The Roman Catholic Council of Trent (1545; adjourned, 1563) established church reforms and strongly stated Roman Catholic theology.

(4) *Conflict* (1562–1598). Religious conflicts marked the closing years of sixteenth-century Europe. The protracted French Wars of Religion began in 1562, and the Dutch Republic struggled for eighty years to gain religious freedom, finally established in 1648, at the end of the Thirty Years' War, the last of Europe's religious wars.

4 What does "Protestant" mean?

The term "Protestant" emerged in relation to the second Diet of Speyer (1529) when a group of princes issued a "protest" (Lat. *protestatio*) against the decision of the diet.

A diet (governmental deliberative assembly) had met at Speyer, Germany, in 1526. The Holy Roman Emperor, Charles V, could not attend. But several princes from northern Germany who were followers of Martin Luther (Lutherans or "evangelicals") were present. The decision of this diet was that each estate in the empire would be allowed to choose between Roman Catholicism and the emerging Lutheran movement. While this would not be a final answer to the future of religion in Germany, further decisions would be made later.

In 1529, King Charles V, desiring to pursue his religious agenda, insisted the diet reconvene, which it did from March 15 through April 22. In the last several years, a number of states had sought to end religious innovations and return to the pre-1517 status on religious matters. Charles demanded the diet revoke the 1526 decision and take steps against the Lutheran movement. This was to prohibit Luther's teachings and put a permanent end to the Reformation. Most German estates supported the king and complied.

But on April 19, 1529, five territories and fourteen south German cities entered an oral *Protestation* (put in writing as an *Appellation* on April 25). This asserted that these parties found the entire transaction of this second Diet of Speyer was null and void and rejected the result. Their *Protestation* was a formal protest or opposition to a decision. But the Latin meaning of the term *protestatio* is from the verb *protestari*, which means "to profess," "to bear witness," or "to declare formally." This is the meaning applicable to the *Protestation* by the princes at Speyer. Here evangelicals who supported Luther made their public witness to support the expression of Christian faith in which they believed and which had claimed their consciences. Their "protest" was their "witness" to this faith. So they came to be called "Protestants."

5 Who were major Protestant Reformers?

Reforming efforts in the Roman Catholic Church and the various Protestant churches that emerged from the Reformation period were the work of many persons. Some of these persons played key roles.

Four major Protestant Reformers of the sixteenth-century Reformation era were Martin Luther (1483–1546), Huldrych Zwingli (1484–1531), John Calvin (1509–1564), and Menno Simons (1496–1561). Each was significant in the formation and development of major confessional traditions associated with emerging church bodies of the period.

Luther was the theologian whose actions initiated the broad Protestant movement and who is most prominently associated with the Protestant Reformation. His views took shape in the Augsburg Confession (1530). "Lutherans" adhered to Luther's theological insights, and Lutherans became a major religious party in the majority of Germany and all Scandinavia.

Zwingli and Calvin were leaders of the "Reformed" theological tradition. Zwingli was in Zurich; Calvin was in Geneva. The Reformed tradition moved beyond Switzerland into Scotland and France, to Hungary and Poland. Both theologians published extensively, and numerous Reformed confessions of faith emerged from the various locations of Reformed churches.

Menno Simons was a former Roman Catholic priest and became a leader of Anabaptists. The Anabaptists were part of the "Radical Reformation," which did not have the backing of ruling civil authorities as did the other three Reformers, in different places. Anabaptist activities were strongest in the Low Countries and at various places from England to Russia. They were frequently persecuted until eventually able to experience toleration in most places.

Other important Protestant Reformers were Philipp Melanchthon (1497–1560), Luther's successor; Heinrich Bullinger (1504–1575), Zwingli's successor; and Theodore Beza (1519–1605), Calvin's successor. The mediating Reformed theologian, Martin Bucer (1491–1551), also played an important role. Other Anabaptist leaders included Balthasar Hubmaier (1485?–1528) and Pilgram Marpeck (c. 1495–1556). In England, in what became the Church of England, leaders included Thomas Cranmer (1489–1556) and Richard Hooker (1554–1600). Among the Puritans, important theologians included Thomas Cartwright (1535–1603) and William Perkins (1558–1602).

Roman Catholic reform leaders included the humanist scholar Desiderius Erasmus (c. 1466–1536) and Ignatius Loyola (1491–1556).

6 What ways did printing help the Reformation?

In the mid-1440s, Johannes Gutenberg (c. 1390–1468), an energetic entrepreneur in Mainz, Germany, began to experiment with ways to mass produce books. His invention of movable type in

1455 moved the production of books away from copying manuscripts by hand to the book form we know today. Gutenberg's first
production was a printed Bible. What was not clear was how the
quantities of books that could now be produced could be sold in
European marketplaces.

When the Reformation began to create a torrent of writings,
led by the vast output of Martin Luther, the early printing industry
evolved as printing took place in numerous cities and towns. The
spread of Luther's writings and ideas—and responses to them—
propelled the Reformation. Theological writings became available
in the vernaculars of people throughout Europe. The Reformation
could not have occurred and proceeded as it did without print.
Broadsheets, pamphlets, books, and printed images all helped
spread the Reformation faith. Luther's writings could be published
swiftly. He had the technological capacity to turn things around
quickly when he wrote about hot topics or crises.

Print propelled Luther. In the fifty years after Luther began publishing, the little town of Wittenberg, where he taught, became a
center of the book world. Luther's writings fostered the growth of
the printing industry; the printing industry was the means by which
Luther's ideas spread throughout Europe and to lands beyond.

Luther's translation of the Bible into German sold quickly and
enabled common people to read the Scriptures in their own language. As literacy rates increased, learning was laicized. Major
theological works, like Melanchthon's *Loci communes* and Calvin's *Institutes of the Christian Religion*, were also published in
numerous editions and became significant parts of Protestantism's
development. At the same time, the printing of pamphlets that
brutally condemned enemies in religious wars was also part of the
legacy of the printing industry. These proceeded along with the
production of devotional literature, prayer books, and hymnals to
deepen the piety of Christian believers.

2

Leading People

7 What did John Wycliffe do?

One of the important forerunners to the sixteenth-century Protestant Reformation was an Oxford University professor, John Wycliffe (c. 1330–1384). Wycliffe raised issues and propounded views that came to have resonance in the reforming movements of the Reformation decades later.

Wycliffe's theological views were based on his conviction that the Bible should be the source of authority for the church's doctrine and for Christian life. This led him to question the authority of the pope. Over time, his criticisms of the papacy and the church's hierarchy grew more pronounced, especially since he also advocated that the political power of the king should be above the pope's in England.

Wycliffe's commitment to Scripture as the church's authority led him to critique other contemporary church views and practices. These included criticisms of monks and monasteries as corrupt, the church's eucharistic theology of transubstantiation (in which the substance of the bread and wine were believed to be changed into the body and blood of Christ) as being unbiblical, and the belief that Scripture is best interpreted by persons of humility, instead of the church's clergy and theologians. He also advocated predestination and rejected clerical celibacy, purgatory, indulgences, and praying to saints.

Wycliffe's focus on Scripture led him to become involved in the translation of the Bible into the vernacular English so that all persons could have access to the wisdom of Scripture. He worked with others and translated from the Latin Vulgate, the Bible of the Roman Church, instead of from Hebrew and Greek versions of Scripture. In the days before the printing press, the "Wycliffe Bible" existed only in manuscripts. After his death, Wycliffe's associates continued to work on the translation.

Wycliffe's Bibles were condemned by the Roman Catholic Church, and on May 4, 1415, the Council of Constance declared Wycliffe a heretic. His works were ordered burned, his body exhumed and burned, and his ashes thrown into the River Swift. Wycliffe's thought gave impetus to Lollardy (see question 24), another important movement.

8 Why was John Huss important?

John Huss, or Jan Hus (c. 1372–1415), was a Czech priest and church reformer whose influence extended to Martin Luther in the sixteenth century. In 1411, Huss was excommunicated, and in 1415 he was condemned, with Wycliffe, by the Council of Constance. Huss's safe conduct was revoked, and he was burned at the stake. His followers were to be suppressed. They fought, resisting five papal crusades between 1420–1431 in the Hussite Wars.

Huss's University of Prague had copies of many of Wycliffe's writings, and in 1402 Huss began to preach and advocate church reform in Bohemia. Among its features were frequent communion and the abolishment of hierarchy and privilege when rich and poor, men and women, stood together to approach the altar for the Eucharist. Huss translated a work of Wycliffe's and published *De ecclesia* (*The Church*) in 1413. The clergy of Prague instigated Huss's arrest, while Huss said the only judge to whom he was responsible was Jesus Christ.

Charges against Huss included his challenging papal primacy and his believing that the pope's power came from the state, instead of from God. Huss claimed that the Bible did not sanction ecclesiastical obedience and that the church's use of excommunication was being improperly overused so that it became a means of oppression.

Huss was condemned as a "noxious son" of Wycliffe, but Huss refused to recant. Followers of Huss in "The Four Articles of Prague" (1420) sought the free preaching of the Word of God, Communion with the reception of both bread and wine, the elimination of the church's secular power, and the punishment of serious sins. A strong focus of Hussites was condemnation of church and secular abuses, including immorality, simony, and social injustice. These were condemned from a deep emphasis on the law of God.

Moderate Hussites prior to the sixteenth-century Reformation founded the Bohemian Brethren, which had affinities with Luther. Their heirs included the Moravians.

9 Why was Girolamo Savonarola important?

Girolamo Savonarola (1452–1498) was a Dominican priest and reformer whose fiery preaching led to his excommunication and execution.

Savonarola was born to a noble family in Ferrara, Italy. He studied medicine and the liberal arts, being influenced by humanism. After a spiritual crisis, he became a Dominican friar and was ordained in 1477. He became known as a biblical scholar. In Florence, he composed philosophical and spiritual works, preaching throughout the city and in the countryside.

Savonarola's message was apocalyptic in nature. He predicted a coming scourge of the church before its restoration. His sermons were personal and direct in force. His popularity soared in 1494 when Charles VIII of France invaded Italy, apparently confirming Savonarola's prediction that a mighty king would invade the country as a judgment on the people's sins.

Savonarola was involved in the nation's politics, and his message became one of preparing the city of Florence for its destiny. He sought reforms but encountered opposition from government and clergy. Savonarola's campaigns featured processions, bonfires of "vanities," and public prayers. But his pro-French policies led to opposition from Pope Alexander VI. Despite being under a ban from the pope, Savonarola continued to preach. He was arrested, tortured, and forced to confess to crimes of false prophecy and political conspiracy before his execution by hanging and burning on May 23, 1498.

Savonarola's preaching inspired others who sought church reform. He preached against clergy corruption, despotic government, and the exploitation of the poor. Luther read some of Savonarola's writings and saw him as a martyr and perhaps as a forerunner of some of Luther's theological insights, particularly justification. In France, Savonarola came to be regarded as a predecessor of the French evangelicals and Huguenot reforms for the French church.

Savonarola's reforming efforts were a prominent example of the crisis of discipline in the medieval church. He and other reformers sought changes. His flaming preaching showed the power of proclamation to ignite the imagination and energies of its hearers.

10 Who was Martin Luther?

Martin Luther (1483–1546) was the most prominent Protestant Reformer whose Ninety-five Theses of October 31, 1517, has traditionally been seen as the public launch of the Protestant Reformation.

Luther was an Augustinian monk who had promised God to become a monk after the experience of a thunderstorm on June 2, 1505, in which he was nearly killed. In the Augustinian monastery, Luther followed the prescriptions of fasting, prayer, and confession. But he could not find the assurance of salvation for which he deeply longed. He was ordained in 1507, sent to teach theology at the University of Wittenberg in 1508, and became a Doctor of Theology in 1512.

Luther's lectures on New Testament books, particularly Romans, led him to a breakthrough of discovering the New Testament message that humans do not gain salvation by obedience to God's law, which is impossible due to sin. Instead humans are justified by faith in Jesus Christ as God's sent Messiah and savior, received by God's grace (Rom. 1:16–17). In his death, Christ has provided for forgiveness and salvation. Humans are declared righteous in God's sight on the basis of Christ's righteousness, and not through trying to gain salvation by doing the good works of obeying the law. Salvation is received, not earned.

Luther's initial critiques of Roman Catholic Church doctrine and practices, beginning with indulgences, led him to develop his theology in light of the cross of Jesus Christ where humanity is saved through Christ's suffering and death. Theology is to be based on the Scriptures as God's Word. Christians are bound together in the church in which they worship God, hear God's Word proclaimed, and participate in the sacraments (baptism and the Lord's Supper). Through faith, Christians are free in God's sight and are also servants of others, expressing their faith through love of others.

Luther's efforts ignited the Reformation. His theological views became influential and widely discussed for centuries to come.

11 Who was Philipp Melanchthon?

Luther's closest associate and fellow theologian was Philipp Melanchthon (1497–1560). He was known as *Praeceptor Germaniae*, the "Teacher of Germany." Melanchthon was educated as a humanist scholar and, though never ordained, brought wide gifts to his work as a reformer, educator, philologist, and textbook author.

Melanchthon was born in Bretten, Germany. He began his university studies at age twelve and received his Master of Arts degree at age seventeen. In 1518, he became Professor of Greek at the newly established University of Wittenberg in Saxony, and in 1520, he married Katherine Krapp, daughter of the city's mayor.

As a colleague of Luther, Melanchthon was captivated by Luther's message and became a skilled interpreter of Scripture and a theologian. In 1521, his *Loci communes* was published. It was a handbook of *commonplaces,* or *common topics,* of theological matters and became a standard textbook for theological students, highly praised by Luther. Melanchthon's commentary on Romans (1522; 1529; and 1532) was widely used as well.

When Luther was an outlaw in the eyes of the government, Melanchthon became the main theological spokesman for emerging Lutheran theology. He presented the Augsburg Confession at the Diet of Augsburg (1530) and later the Apology for the Augsburg Confession (1531), which sharpened the focus of the confession.

Melanchthon spent decades working in the politics of church reform, seeking to spread the evangelical faith and to work with Reformed church leaders. His *Confessio Augustana variata* (1540) sought to build bridges and was a document to which John Calvin assented. But he was criticized by other followers of Luther, and in his final years he sought intra-Lutheran harmony. Melanchthon contributed much to the Lutheran movement. He kept to its theological insights while also trying to find ways to navigate difficult political, social, and ecclesiastical waters for the sake of Christ's church.

12 Who was Huldrych Zwingli?

It's hard to imagine a name further down on an alphabetical list than "Zwingli"!

Huldrych Zwingli (1484–1531) began the Protestant Reformation in Switzerland. As a Roman Catholic priest, trained in humanism and influenced by Erasmus, Zwingli served in Glarus where he studied the Bible and early church theologians.

Zwingli began doubting Roman Catholic doctrine and practices. He criticized unbiblical practices of adoration of saints and relics and, like Luther, indulgences.

Yet Zwingli became priest at the Grossmünster ("Great Cathedral") in Zurich. On January 1, 1519 (his thirty-fifth birthday), Zwingli began sermons on the Gospel of Matthew, basing them on the Greek New Testament text rather than on the Latin Vulgate translation authorized by the Roman church.

Zwingli began to read Luther's writings and became a follower. He attacked abuses in the church, fasting, confession of sins to a priest, the celibacy of the clergy, the Roman Mass, and monasticism. He also stripped the churches of pictures and icons and—though an accomplished musician—forbade the use of music in church services. With the support of the city council and against church practice, he allowed meat to be eaten during Lent.

The council also supported Zwingli's Sixty-seven Theses, debated on January 29, 1523. It withdrew the Zurich canton from the jurisdiction of the Bishop of Constance, officially sanctioning Zwingli's Reformation. A Reformed worship service was instituted. The reforms swept through other Swiss churches, next to follow being Basel under the leadership of Johann Oecolampadius (1482–1531).

Despite agreements on a number of theological points at the Colloquy of Marburg (1529), Zwingli and Luther disagreed on the presence of Christ in the Lord's Supper. This was an ongoing contention that prevented the uniting of Reformed and Lutheran churches. Zwingli's followers were "Zwinglians," who had a distinctive theology among other Reformed positions and rejected Luther's view of the real presence of Christ in the Lord's Supper.

Zwingli was killed on the battlefield in the Second Battle of Kappel, waged against the Roman Catholics, who had Zwingli's body drawn and quartered and burned.

13 Who was Heinrich Bullinger?

Zwingli's successor as the lead pastor (*antistes*) in Zurich was Heinrich Bullinger (1504–1575). This Swiss-German reformer began his ministry in Zurich five years before Calvin came to Geneva and was still in ministry eleven years after Calvin's death. His extensive theological writings, correspondence, and pastoral leadership made him an important and influential reformer.

After study at the University of Cologne, Bullinger became interested in theology and studied Luther's works of 1520 and Melanchthon's *Loci communes*. By 1522, he was an evangelical Christian. Bullinger became head teacher at a Cistercian monastery at Kappel where he wrote many New Testament commentaries and lectured from them. The monastery was reformed. In 1523, Bullinger met Zwingli and became associated with the Zurich reformer. After succeeding his father as pastor at Bremgarten (1529), Bullinger and his family fled after Zurich troops lost Kappel and arrived in Zurich on November 21, 1531. On December 13, he replaced Zwingli as the lead pastor.

Bullinger built on Zwingli's theological foundation but moved beyond him on several important matters. Bullinger's treatise *De testamento* (*The One and Eternal Testament or Covenant*, 1534) had long-lasting effect. His *Decades* (1549) was a collection of fifty sermons that covered major Christian doctrines. Bullinger wrote the First Helvetic Confession (1536) and the Second Helvetic Confession (1566), the latter being a comprehensive doctrinal confession and the most widely used of the early Reformed confessions of faith.

Bullinger and Calvin had extensive correspondence and were able to forge an agreement with the Consensus Tigurinus (Zurich Agreement, 1549). Bullinger saw the Lord's Supper as a *testimony* of God's grace, while Calvin saw it as an *instrument* of God's grace. The consensus omitted instrumental language. Bullinger's teachings on predestination emphasized God's grace in electing to eternal life. His theology was marked by an emphasis on sanctification, the Christian's growth in grace. He emphasized the Christian's duty to love others and do good works, always exhorting believers to live the Christian life.

 **Who was Martin Bucer?**

Martin Bucer (1491–1551) was an important reformer in Strasbourg who helped shape the Reformed tradition in key directions.

Bucer was born to a humble family in Alsace, Germany. He became a Dominican friar in his hometown, being educated by the Dominicans but also being influenced by Erasmus and other humanists. Bucer studied at Heidelberg and attended Luther's disputation there (1518), leading him to become a convinced follower. He was released from his monastic vows in 1521 and became a parish pastor and married a former nun.

After being excommunicated (1523), Bucer fled to Strasbourg where he lectured on the Bible, becoming a pastor in 1524. Along with his colleague, Wolfgang Capito (c. 1478–1541), Bucer worked for church reform and became an active theological voice through his writings. In 1529, he attended the Colloquy of Marburg as a representative of the Reformed. This began his efforts to bring the Zwinglians and Lutherans together.

Bucer played a significant role in influencing John Calvin when Calvin served a French refugee church and lectured in the Academy at Strasbourg. Here Calvin saw a Reformed church order with church discipline, contemplated predestination, and the Lord's Supper, while especially imbibing the importance of worship and liturgy, ordered church ministries, and the importance of education, along with Bucer's vision of a Christian society.

Bucer's ecumenical work featured participation in the Regensburg Colloquy (1541) where he helped structure an agreement on justification by faith between Protestants and Catholics. But other aspects of the Colloquy's work were rejected by the Catholics, and Bucer's efforts did not bear fruit.

When the Protestants were defeated by imperial forces in 1549, Bucer accepted Thomas Cranmer's invitation to come to England, where he lectured at the University of Cambridge. Bucer impacted Church of England Protestantism in the area of worship and also submitted a guide for national reform to King Edward VI with his *The Kingdom of Christ* (1557). Bucer continued to teach theology at Cambridge until his death. His attempts at mediating Protestant positions helped make him a significant leader.

15 Who was Katharina Schütz Zell?

Katharina Schütz Zell (c. 1497–1562) was a reformer and activist in Strasbourg for over forty years. She was the daughter of a cabinetmaker and received a middle-class education. She wrote

German well and published five treatises. She and a circle of her friends were converted to the evangelical faith by reading the early writings of Luther, with whom Zell established a correspondence.

Her marriage to Matthias Zell (1477–1548), one of the four important Strasbourg reformers, led to Matthias's excommunication. She wrote a pamphlet defending the validity of clergy marriages.

Zell had a strong sense of vocation to spread the evangelical faith. She maintained an open house to welcome visiting reformers and refugees and spent energies in organizing food and shelter for many people in need, especially for victims of the Peasants' War (1525). She was prominent in the city and gave the eulogy at her husband's funeral.

Zell's hospitality to the otherwise "unwelcomed" included Anabaptists and her friend Caspar Schwenckfeld (1490–1561), a spiritualist who had settled in Strasbourg. This led Zell to be called a "disturber of the peace of the church" by the city's Lutheran clergy.

The range and scope of her publications were notable for her time and situation. Her first pamphlet (1524) consoled women separated from their husbands because of the Protestant faith. Her piece on clerical marriage was addressed to the local bishop. From 1534–1536, Zell wrote the preface for four small booklets of hymns. An autobiographical exchange of letters with a Lutheran pastor (1557) was followed by her final publication (1558): devotional meditations on some psalms, the Lord's Prayer, and the Apostles' Creed. The manuscript of her sermon at her husband's funeral also survives.

Though Zell was suspected of heresy, no one ever produced proof, and upon her death, she was buried according to the Lutheran burial rite. Zell had defended the dissidents and called for toleration for Roman Catholics and Anabaptists, and after the Marburg Colloquy (1529), she wrote to urge Luther to let Christian love overcome his theological hostilities.

16 Who was Guillaume (William) Farel?

Guillaume (William) Farel (1489–1565) was a French Reformed pastor and theologian. He was the chief minister in Geneva who was instrumental in persuading John Calvin to begin his ministry there in 1536.

Farel studied under the leading humanist, Jacques Lefèvre d'Étaples (c. 1455–1536), and became a lay evangelist in Meaux, France, under a reformist bishop. But when the pace of reform was too slow, Farel left Meaux in 1524 and spent ten years preaching throughout the Rhine valley and French-speaking Switzerland. He helped bring Protestantism to Geneva in 1532. By 1535–1536, Farel led the city to accept the Protestant faith and looked to the task of further reforms.

Due to a battle that forced Calvin to reroute his journey with a stop in Geneva, he intended to stay there one night. But when Farel heard he was in town—Calvin being an up-and-coming theologian and author of the *Institutes of the Christian Religion* (1536)—he confronted Calvin to invite (command!) him to stay and help with the reform. Calvin wanted a quieter life. But the red-haired, fiery Farel thundered that God would curse his labors if he did not obey. Calvin obeyed.

From 1536 to April 1538, Farel and Calvin led the Geneva church in new, Protestant directions. A dispute with the Genevan authorities over the Lord's Supper led to their banishment from the city. Calvin went to Strasbourg but returned to Geneva in 1541. Farel became a pastor in Neuchâtel where he had initiated the Reformation in 1530. He stayed there for the rest of his life.

For years, Farel was the preeminent French-speaking Protestant theologian. He wrote the first French Reformation tract (1524), the first extensive work on Reformed doctrine in French (*Summaire et briefve declaration*, c. 1529), and the first French Reformed liturgy (*La maniere et fasson*, 1533 but perhaps 1528). Yet Farel recognized Calvin's gifts and supported his ministries. Farel's impulsive temperament was suited to initiating reforms. But he was also able to see the gifts of others and enlist them in reforming causes. Farel is rightly called the "Father of the French Reformation."

17 Who was John Calvin?

John Calvin (1509–1564) was the leading reformer for what became the Reformed theological tradition. Calvin's followers were called "Calvinists." Calvin's was a primary, though not the only, voice in establishing alternative theological understandings to Luther's views.

Calvin was born in Picardy in Noyon, France, and began to study for the priesthood until his father determined that he should become a lawyer. When his father died, Calvin switched back to studying the liberal arts. Through studies at a variety of universities, Calvin was introduced to humanism.

Probably in 1533, Calvin experienced a "conversion" and became an evangelical Protestant through study of Luther's thought. Calvin fled Paris in 1534 and left France to settle in Basel before being enjoined to work with William Farel in instituting the Protestant reform in Geneva in 1536. After Calvin and Farel were expelled from Geneva in 1538, due to a dispute with the city government, Calvin became a pastor to French refugees in Strasbourg where he was associated with Martin Bucer. Calvin was called back to Geneva in 1541 and spent the remainder of his years there as the city's leading pastor, theologian, and author. He became an international figure. His concerns in Geneva were extensive, including education and relief of the poor.

Calvin's writings were wide-ranging. His *Institutes of the Christian Religion*, developing Latin and French versions from 1536–1560, was his main theological treatise and became a classic. Calvin wrote commentaries on most biblical books, his *Institutes* expressing theologically what Calvin interpreted the Scriptures to mean.

Calvin is often associated with the doctrine of election or predestination. He saw this as an expression of salvation by God's grace as a free gift to sinners. The church is the "elect of God," those who have been given the gift of faith in Jesus Christ by the work of the Holy Spirit. Calvin's strong emphasis was on God's initiative in doing for sinners what they cannot do for themselves—being forgiven of sin and being established in a relationship of trust and love with God through Jesus Christ.

18 Who was John Knox?

John Knox (c. 1514–1572) was the leading reformer in Scotland, known as the founder of Scottish Presbyterianism.

Knox was ordained a Roman Catholic priest (1536) but was converted to Protestantism and called as a preacher in St. Andrews, Scotland. When the castle of St. Andrews fell to French forces, the Protestant Knox was imprisoned as a galley slave in France for nineteen months. On his release (1549), he was a preacher in England and a chaplain to King Edward VI. When the Roman Catholic Mary Tudor became Queen of England (1553), Knox was driven into exile. In 1555 he was in Geneva where he studied under Calvin, was a pastor for refugees, and wrote works attacking Roman Catholicism and urging the overthrow of Catholic leaders. Knox was also a pastor in Frankfurt where he was involved in a controversy over worship practices.

Knox was called back to Scotland in 1559. He was active in preaching and pressing the cause for Protestant reforms in the country. In 1560, Knox and his associates wrote the Scots Confession and *The First Book of Discipline* (1561), which were approved by Parliament and established a presbyterian form of church government in the land. The pope's authority was abolished, and celebrations of the Mass became illegal. Knox was often in controversy with the Catholic queen, Mary Queen of Scots, who returned to rule Scotland from 1561 to 1567. Knox was minister of St. Giles in Edinburgh and the nation's leading preacher.

Knox wrote *The First Blast of the Trumpet against the Monstrous Regiment of Women* (1558), arguing against the rule of women, particularly in England and Scotland. His *The History of the Reformation of Religion in Scotland* (1586–1587) related the events of the Scottish Reformation.

Knox's theological emphases were on the authority of Scripture and God's sovereignty. The church is those chosen and called by God. It is marked by the preaching of the Word, the right administration of the sacraments, and ecclesiastical discipline. The mark of "discipline" had not been part of Calvin's definition of the marks of the church. But it was especially prominent in the Scottish Presbyterian context.

19 Who was Menno Simons?

Menno Simons (1496–1561) was a Roman Catholic priest who became an Anabaptist and led a nonviolent group of Dutch Anabaptists. His followers became known as Mennonites.

Menno began to doubt the Roman Catholic doctrine of transubstantiation, in which the elements in the Eucharist become the body and blood of Jesus Christ. When the reformer Melchior Hoffman (c. 1495–1543) began baptizing adults, Menno found he could establish no support for infant baptism. By 1534, his thought was moving toward Hoffman's "Melchiorite" views.

Saddened by the tragedy at Münster where many Anabaptists were killed (1535; see question 29), which he repudiated, Menno left his priesthood to lead remnants of Anabaptists away from violent viewpoints. In a year, he was baptized and ordained an elder by the Anabaptist leader, Obbe Philips (c. 1500–1568) in the winter of 1536–1537. This led him to a persecuted life for twenty-five years, seeking to avoid being apprehended by the law for his Anabaptist views. He was declared a fugitive by King Charles V in 1542. In 1561, Menno died and was buried in his cabbage garden.

Menno gave leadership to Anabaptists, becoming their major figure. He taught a life of Christian discipleship, beginning with adult baptism. Saved persons must do good works of the law as a demonstration of the reality of their faith. Believers should seek to take on the perfection of Jesus Christ in their lives of faith.

The Anabaptist Schleitheim Articles (1527) had taught the

doctrine of the ban—that those disciples in the community who fell into sin should be excluded from the community. Menno advocated this vigorously. There was no hope of establishing a broad "Christian society" since the wider culture would not practice the strict standards Menno believed were truly Christian. So Mennonites defined themselves in opposition to prevailing cultures and society practices. The church has only spiritual weapons; and should never practice violence. True power was in pacifism and not warfare.

20 Who was William Tyndale?

William Tyndale (c. 1494–1536) was an English biblical translator and theologian. His theological views were a combination of diverse emphases emerging from early Protestant debates on the European continent.

Tyndale was born in Gloucestershire and educated at Oxford University. He became acquainted with the works of Erasmus and from his personal experiences believed the best hope for reform of the English church was from the Bible, translated into the vernacular of the English people.

The English church hierarchy opposed a vernacular translation since this was associated with the heresies of John Wycliffe and his Lollard followers. So Tyndale left for Germany in 1524 and in a year had completed translating the New Testament from Greek. It was the first New Testament translated from Greek and printed in English. Tyndale had a strong knowledge of Greek, taught himself Hebrew, and was talented at writing memorable English. His work drew on Luther's understandings and reflected these in the translation. The book was published in Worms, Germany (1526), and after copies were smuggled into England, they were burned by English authorities.

For the next ten years, Tyndale was in hiding and worked on translating the Old Testament. He was captured in 1535 by the Dutch after having produced a revised New Testament. In 1536, Tyndale was burned at the stake near Brussels. A Bible based on

Tyndale's work was published in 1535 and a legalized version appeared in 1537. Tyndale's translations helped form a basis for the English language King James Bible published in 1611 with its New Testament featuring 90 percent of Tyndale's words and syntax.

Tyndale's theology emphasized justification by faith and also was heavily influenced by his view of biblical covenants. He defended royal authority against the papacy in *The Obedience of a Christian Man* (1528).

21 Who was King Henry VIII?

Henry Tudor (1491–1547) became heir to the English throne on the death of his brother Arthur in 1502 and became king on April 22, 1509. He married Catherine of Aragon, a Spanish princess and his brother's widow, on June 11, 1509.

Henry VIII lived on a large scale, seeking to become a ruler of power and magnificence. Religiously, Henry published a defense of the traditional Roman Catholic understanding of the sacraments (1521, probably aided by Thomas More [1478–1535]) when Luther's views began to be noticed. Pope Leo X named him *Fidei Defensor*, "Defender of the Faith."

Only one child of Henry and Catherine survived to adulthood, Princess Mary (later, as the Roman Catholic Queen, known as "Bloody Mary"). Henry was convinced his marriage to Catherine violated divine law and was invalid, so he sought an annulment from Pope Clement VII with a papal dispensation to marry Anne Boleyn. The question was prolonged from 1527 through 1529.

When Anne became pregnant (daughter, Elizabeth, who reigned 1558 to 1603), an urgency to have the matter settled developed. Henry turned to the cleric, Thomas Cranmer (1489–1556), who suggested that Henry did not need to wait for an annulment. Cranmer was made Archbishop of Canterbury and presided over Henry and Anne's marriage (1533). When the pope threatened to excommunicate Henry, Parliament passed an Act of Supremacy (1534), which declared the king of England, and not the pope, as the head of the English church.

With Henry as head of the Church, the English Reformation had begun. But the country did not move into fully Protestant directions. Henry's views were conservative, and he maintained a strong attachment to the real presence of Christ in the Mass, the celibate priesthood, and the importance of "good works" for salvation. He also executed mainstream Protestants, leading a number of Protestants to seek refuge on the continent. Henry did, however, dissolve monasteries and ban veneration of idols, and when the "Great Bible" was published (1539), its frontispiece displayed Henry handing out the Bible to church leaders. So Henry himself was a religious enigma. But he saw his role of king as blending seamlessly with his role as head of the church.

22 Who was Thomas Cranmer?

Thomas Cranmer (1489–1556) was a complex figure who was appointed by King Henry VIII of England as the ecclesiastical head of the English church, Archbishop of Canterbury (1533).

Cranmer graduated from Jesus College of the University of Cambridge, and in 1526, he received a Doctor of Divinity degree and was ordained a priest. In 1529, Cranmer began to work for Henry VIII to produce propaganda in favor of Henry's divorce so that he could marry Anne Boleyn. In 1532, Henry named him Archbishop, and he was consecrated on March 30, 1533.

By this time, Cranmer had become an evangelical, his having married the niece of a Lutheran pastor Andreas Osiander, while Cranmer was on a diplomatic mission. Henry believed Cranmer would support his divorce unconditionally. Cranmer annulled Henry's marriage and officiated at his wedding to Anne Boleyn.

Cranmer cautiously worked for the evangelical cause and did Henry's bidding. He instituted some liturgical forms, maintaining Henry's trust. When Henry's young son Edward VI became King (1547), Cranmer led full-fledged Protestant reforms. He welcomed the reformer Martin Bucer to England, wrote a treatise on the Lord's Supper, and drew up doctrinal articles for the English church. He was the principal author of the *Book of Common*

Prayer (1549), which led to widespread liturgical reform. Cranmer was interested in uniting Protestant churches and held a broadly Reformed theology.

The archbishop opposed the accession of Mary I ("Bloody Mary"), who had him imprisoned for treason and heresy. Dispirited in prison, Cranmer signed a series of recantations. But Mary still ordered him burnt at the stake in Oxford (1556). Cranmer thrust his right hand into the flames so that it would burn first, thus dramatically symbolizing his rejection of the recantations he had signed with that hand. To the end, he maintained a Protestant allegiance.

23 Who was Ignatius of Loyola?

Ignatius of Loyola (c. 1491–1556) was a Roman Catholic reformer and founder of the Society of Jesus (Jesuits). His influence was strong and long-lasting. He revolutionized Roman Catholic evangelism, founded schools, and sought to maintain Roman Catholic orthodoxy.

Ignatius was born to a noble family in the Spanish castle of Loyola. After becoming a soldier, his right leg was shattered in the battle of Pamplona against the French in 1521. In a long recuperation, Ignatius read spiritual books, including stories of lives of the saints. His life was transformed so that he wished to seek God's glory. His deep spiritual and mystical experiences led to his writing the *Spiritual Exercises,* which became the core book of Jesuit spirituality and which Ignatius revised throughout the next quarter century.

Though Ignatius desired to convert Muslims in Jerusalem, he realized he needed education. He learned Latin at a boy's school in Barcelona and went on to the universities of Alcala and Salamanca, then to the University of Paris (1528–1535). Six students gathered round him, including Francis Xavier (1506–1552) who became a missionary to India and Japan. These formed the nucleus of the Society of Jesus, and most of the six were ordained as priests in 1537. Pope Paul III recognized them as an Order of the church in 1540.

Ignatius functioned in Roman Catholicism as Luther did in Protestantism. He was a master organizer who saw the church's problem as discipline. His Order emphasized obedience to the church. His *Spiritual Exercises* became a basis for the spiritual lives of thousands. Jesuit missionaries took Christianity to the new world with missionary zeal. The Jesuits opened schools, and education became the primary Jesuit ministry.

Jesuit theologians were prominent at the Council of Trent (1545–1563) and increasingly took on the mission of countering the Protestant Reformation.

3

Events and Developments

24 Who were the Lollards?

Lollards gained their impetus from the work of John Wycliffe. They spread and popularized Wycliffe's views, positions considered heretical by the Roman Catholic Church. From the late fourteenth century, the term "Lollard" (or "Wycliffite") labeled theologians and preachers as heretics. The term was linked to the Latin word *lolia*, meaning "weeds," bringing to mind Jesus' parable of the tares (weeds) among the good grain (Matt. 13:24–30).

Lollardy was a movement that was decidedly anticlerical in character. It encompassed a diverse range of beliefs and actions that were perceived to threaten the established religious authorities. Central was a concern for the use of English for studying the Bible, as well as theological discussions of established church practices.

Lollardy was a movement of the common people. Lollards perpetuated Wycliffe's views and used his English Bible to critique traditional Roman Catholic teachings. They found in Scripture justifications for castigating the great wealth of the church and came to believe individual Christians could function as priests. This priesthood of the laity meant the sacrament of penance and oral confession of sins to the church's ordained priests was not necessary. Confession was to be made to Christ alone.

After 1401, English authorities persecuted Lollards, who could be tried for heresy and burnt. This meant Lollardy became a largely underground movement, living by Bible study and preaching.

Translated Bibles were outlawed, especially those that featured a preface by a Wycliffe sympathizer. Ownership of such a Bible was a way to mark a Lollard.

Lollardy helped bring the Scriptures and theological discourse into the lives of common people in England. Sermons stressed the need to imitate Christ in daily life, live Christian lives of faith, and serve God through good works, motivated by the Holy Spirit and guided by the Word of God with the help of the sacraments.

25 What happened at the Diet of Worms?

On June 15, 1520, Pope Leo X issued a bull, or proclamation, *Exsurge Domine* (*Arise, O Lord*), condemning Luther's writings, specifically forty-one of Luther's Ninety-five Theses. It threatened that Luther would be excommunicated unless he recanted or denounced his views within sixty days. Luther refused. Instead, he issued a series of writings against the papacy. On December 10, 1520, Martin Luther publicly burned the pope's proclamation.

In January 1521, Luther was excommunicated from the church. Theologian Johann Eck (1486–1543), with whom Luther had debated at Leipzig in 1519, demanded King Charles V, the Holy Roman Emperor, join with the pope against Luther. Charles summoned Luther to the Diet (legislative assembly) meeting in the city of Worms in southwestern Germany to answer for his opinions. Luther was promised safe conduct to the city and was met by cheering throngs. He was fully aware of the dangers but later said he would have gone to Worms even if there were "as many devils in it as there were tiles on the roofs of the houses."

Luther appeared before the delegates on April 17, 1521. He was ordered to recant his views. He asked for a day to contemplate. But the next day he refused to retract his published views. He famously answered that unless he was convinced by "Scripture or by clear reason," he was bound by the Scriptures and his conscience was "captive to the Word of God." So he could not or would not recant anything, because he could not go against his conscience. He concluded: "God help me. Amen." According to tradition, before saying, "God help me," Luther said, "Here I stand, I can do no other." Though it may be doubtful Luther said, "Here I stand," the phrase symbolizes Luther's courage in the face of uncertainties and potential death.

26 What did Luther do when hiding in Wartburg Castle?

After Luther refused to recant his theological views at the Diet of Worms, he left the city secretly on April 26, 1521. On May 25, Charles V signed the Edict of Worms, a decree declaring Luther an outlaw. Though his safe conduct was being honored, Luther was a wanted man. He was to be arrested. No one could legally shelter him, and his books could not be printed, sold, or read.

While returning to Wittenberg, Luther was told on May 3 that his "abduction" would soon occur. Luther released the officer charged with providing the imperial safe conduct. The next day masked horsemen appeared from the Thuringian Forest and commanded Luther to identify himself. Then they grabbed him and made him run beside them until they were out of sight. The kidnapping was arranged by Elector Frederick the Wise. Luther was taken to Wartburg Castle, overlooking the city of Eisenach.

There, Luther lived safely for nearly a year, letting his hair grow, jettisoning his monk's habit, and masquerading as "Knight George." He spent his time translating the New Testament from Greek into German. This he did in ten weeks and the New Testament was published in 1522. Luther used Erasmus's second edition of the Greek New Testament (1519) instead of the Latin Vulgate, the official version of the Roman Catholic Church. During this time, Luther went into towns and markets to listen to the common people speaking so that he could translate the Scriptures in the ways the people used the German language. In 1534, with the help of others, Luther's complete German Bible was published.

One feature of Luther's New Testament translation was that at Romans 3:28, Luther added the word "alone" (Lat. *sola*, Germ. *allein*) after "faith." Today this is translated, "For we hold that a person is justified by faith [alone] apart from works prescribed by the law" (NRSV). Luther argued that the addition was correct because it was needed by colloquial German and also accorded with Paul's intended meaning. "Faith alone" became a slogan of Luther, capturing the way by which salvation comes to humans in Jesus Christ.

27 What was the Peasants' Revolt?

The Peasants' Revolt (War; now sometimes called the Revolution of the Common Man) was a series of uprising in Germany in 1524 and 1525. These were begun by peasants, farmers, and common laborers and were embraced by others who wanted a wider social equality. A question is to what degree the teachings of Luther played a part in stirring desires for changes in economic and social conditions.

The lot of peasants in German society was difficult. Those at the lowest end of the social ladder struggled to maintain their existence and provide for their families. Escalating demands for increases in rents, dues, fees, taxes, services, and tithe—from feudal lords and the church—heightened pressures. The required church tithe and the situation of serfdom were the strongest grievances. Radical religious ideas being spread linked acceptance of the gospel with the redress of societal grievances and issues of social justice.

In spring 1524, peasants began to rebel in the counties of Lupfen and Stühlingen and marched on Waldshut. Then the revolt spread. A battle at Frankenhausen involved the spiritual leader of the peasants, Thomas Müntzer, against the Catholic/Lutheran army led by Philip of Hesse. When Philip offered a negotiated peace, the peasants saw a rainbow in the sky. Müntzer had designed two war symbols for the peasants, one being a rainbow on a white banner. The rainbow's appearance was a sign to the peasants that God was with them. So they refused the offer of peace. But this led to Philip's troops slaughtering the peasants. Müntzer was captured and beheaded on May 25, 1525.

Initially, Luther saw the peasants' concerns as God's judgment on unjust rulers. With princes demanding his allegiance, Luther's views of the need to submit to civil authorities on civil matters led him to react vehemently against the Peasants' Revolt. With inflamed and very violent language, Luther wrote *Against the Robbing and Murdering Hordes of Peasants* and urged the German princes to be "God's sword on earth" and put down the revolt. At Frankenhausen, more than six thousand peasants were killed and more than one hundred thousand died throughout the battles. Luther's response, which he later deeply regretted, led many in southern Germany to turn away from Lutheranism to more radical expressions of Christian faith.

28 What was the Radical Reformation?

Historians speak of the "Magisterial Reformation" and the "Radical Reformation."

The "Magisterial Reformation" describes the reforming movements of the Lutherans (following Luther) and the Reformed (following Zwingli and Calvin) and the Church of England (later, Anglicans) in England. These were movements that were endorsed and even established by magistrates or ruling civil authorities in different territories.

The "Radical Reformation" describes reformers and reforming groups—churches, communes, sects, and others—who were not part of the territorial churches of the three major confessional traditions. This grouping has sometimes been called the "Left Wing of the Reformation." There was not one central figure who led the "radicals." Major leaders were Balthasar Hubmaier (c. 1481–1528), Thomas Münster (c. 1489–1525), Melchior Hoffman (c. 1495–1543), Pilgram Marpeck (c. 1495–1556), and Menno Simons (1496–1561).

Among those in this wing of the Reformation, there was a strong desire to form a pure Christian community, emphasizing discipleship as a defining feature of what it means to be a Christian, and to recognize Christian life as living against cultural norms and being "separate" from the prevailing society. A common bond was rejection of infant baptism. Adult or "believers baptism" was to be the norm in this "ordinance" (not a sacrament). "Anabaptists" (from *ana,* which in Greek means "again") was originally a name of reproach for those in this group who practiced "rebaptism" (baptism again) of those who had been "baptized" as infants—not recognizing infant baptism as a valid expression of Christian confession or discipleship.

Those in Radical Reformation movements did not develop a formal or systematic theology. They recognized suffering as a badge of Christian life, their movements and leaders being persecuted throughout Europe. They lived outside official churches, developing their spirituality and life in the church in distinctive ways that reflected their strong Christian commitments.

29 What happened to Anabaptists in Müntser?

While the Peasants' War led many Anabaptists to turn to separation from the world and pacifism as indicated by the Schleitheim Articles (1527), not all did so.

Apocalyptic preaching was a mark of Melchior Hoffman, who was not a priest or educated theologian. In Wittenberg, Hoffman proclaimed himself a lay preacher, but after getting into trouble in several cities for inciting religious unrest, Hoffman baptized several hundred people and began several churches in East Frisia, Germany. He saw himself as a new prophet and declared that before Christ returned to earth, all ungodly persons would be removed from the earth—a message that alerted civic authorities to potential dangers. He was jailed in Strasbourg and died at some time near the end of 1543.

But Hoffman's thought inspired followers such as Dirk and Obbe Philips and Menno Simons. Some disciples used his ideas and sought to establish a holy kingdom in Münster. Two leaders there, John of Leiden and a charismatic baker, Jan Matthijs of Haarlem, came to the city to avoid persecution of Anabaptists in the Netherlands. They taught that a new Jerusalem would be established in Münster, a city in northwest Germany. This led in the city to the establishment of a communal way of life and the exodus of all non-Anabaptists. In response an army of Catholic and Lutheran forces encircled the city. Matthijs was killed in action. John of Leiden established a new law code making the city a theocracy where one could be executed for swearing. He declared mandatory polygamy (and took sixteen wives) and had himself crowned Münster's king in September 1534.

But still under siege, the city saw its food supply run low, and the city fell on June 25, 1535. Nearly all inhabitants were killed, with leaders tortured, their bodies put in a cage and hung from the steeple of the church (the cage remaining until the twentieth century).

From this, some Anabaptists saw the tragedy as the result of humans seeking earthly power. For others, it showed that violence led to violence and pacifism was the only legitimate Christian position.

30 What was the Colloquy of Marburg?

The Colloquy of Marburg was called by Landgrave Philip of Hesse to meet in his castle in Marburg. Major leaders of the Reformation were invited with the hope of promoting theological agreements and political harmony among the various groups.

The Colloquy was held on October 1 through October 4, 1529, with the Germans (Lutherans) being led by Martin Luther and Philipp Melanchthon and the Swiss (Reformed) by Huldrych Zwingli, Johann Oecolampadius, and Martin Bucer. The two sides agreed on fourteen of the fifteen propositions proposed. These included agreements on the Trinity, the person of Christ, justification by faith, infant baptism, and the rejection of the Roman Catholic view of transubstantiation—that the elements in the Lord's Supper change in substance to become the body and blood of Jesus Christ. The point of disagreement was on the nature of Christ's presence in the Lord's Supper.

Luther repeatedly attacked Zwingli's views. Luther wrote on the table the words of institution (1 Cor. 11:24), which in Latin are: *Hoc est corpus meum* ("This is my body"). From this Luther would not budge. Luther interpreted the saying literally. Zwingli interpreted the "is" to mean "represents" or "signifies my body" (*significat*). No language or theology could bridge the gap between the two sides on this issue. In the end, Luther said to Zwingli and the others: "If your spirit and our spirit are not in harmony, it is obvious that we do not have the same spirit."

The breakdown in the two camps meant a widening split between Lutheran and Reformed churches. No middle ground could be found. The differences in the issue of the presence of Christ in the Supper pointed also to differences in Christology, the person of Jesus Christ. The summit meeting that was supposed to unite emerging Protestants became the place where a theological difference became an issue that contributed to the widening of two Protestant traditions.

31 What was the Inquisition?

The Inquisition (from the Latin *inquisitio* and the verb meaning "to inquire"; also called the Holy Office) began in the thirteenth century but became newly important during the sixteenth-century Reformation period. Prior to the Reformation, the Inquisition was an institution of the Roman Catholic Church that took distinctive shapes in various regions. Its intention was to monitor and enforce the correctness of religious beliefs among the people.

In Spain, King Ferdinand and Queen Isabella established an Inquisition to confront Jews, especially those who were Roman Catholic converts, and ascertain whether they had really renounced their Jewish views and practices. In 1492 and 1502, royal decrees ordered Jews and Muslims to convert to Roman Catholicism or leave the country. When Protestants emerged in Spain, the Spanish Inquisition focused on rooting out all heresy. This activity was led by a Grand Inquisitor. The organizer of the Spanish Inquisition was Friar Tomás de Torquemada (1420–1498). Those convicted by the Inquisition tribunal of unrepentant heresy were handed over to secular authorities for punishment. Torture was a method of seeking recantation of heretical views.

In the 1540s, Pope Paul III was concerned about the spread of Reformation ideas in Italy and established the Congregation of the Inquisition, known as the Roman Inquisition, which began in 1542. The purpose of the Roman Inquisition was to maintain Roman Catholic orthodoxy. Heresy was considered treason against God and a punishable capital offense. The Holy Office was presided over by the pope and six cardinals who deliberated in secret. Its most notable trial was of Galileo Galilei in 1633, who was condemned for his (Copernican) view that the sun was at the center of the universe. This was deemed heretical and contrary to Holy Scripture. Galileo was placed under house arrest for the remainder of his life.

It is estimated that approximately 3,000 persons were executed by the Spanish Inquisition; around 1,000 in the Portuguese Inquisition; and perhaps 150 in the Roman Inquisition. Torture and death by burning at the stake were instruments of the Inquisition, which accomplished its purposes of repressing Protestantism. Protestant literature helped instill fear of the Inquisition among Protestant believers.

32 What was the Council of Trent?

The nineteenth General Council of the Roman Catholic Church was held in several assemblies from 1545 to 1563. It fostered changes within the church and established Catholic doctrine and practices for centuries.

Politics prevented the Roman church from convening a general council of the church since the indulgence controversy and Luther's theses set things in motion in 1517. Pope Paul III called for the council in 1542, hoping the unity of the church could be restored. This hope was lost. Emphasis became on combating Protestant theology and renewing the Catholic Church.

The three assemblies that met in the Italian town of Trent were 1545–1547, 1551–1552, and 1561–1563. Answers to Protestant critiques were given.

On the authority of Scripture and tradition, Trent affirmed

authority for the church was found in the Scriptures and the unwritten traditions of the church, with the church being the interpreter of Scripture.

On the justification of the sinner, Trent condemned Luther's justification by faith alone. Human merit can move toward justification, the human will doing what it can to accept God's grace. No one could be justified who did not accept this doctrine.

On the sacraments, Trent affirmed Jesus Christ instituted seven sacraments, necessary for salvation. It affirmed the truth of the hierarchical priesthood of the church and that ordination confers an indelible character on the new priest. Protestant views of the Eucharist or Lord's Supper were anathematized and transubstantiation was affirmed.

In its final assembly, the council looked to matters of the church's ongoing life. It affirmed church teaching that in Communion laity should receive only the bread (communion in one kind). It also defined the sacramental character of marriage and clerical celibacy, as well as affirming teachings on purgatory, indulgences, and the veneration of saints. Bishops were defined as pastors, to be concerned with the salvation of souls. Reforming actions included decrees on the formation of seminaries, reform of clergy morals, the preaching of sermons, and a strengthening of the position of the pope in the church.

33 What was the Peace of Augsburg?

After the Second Diet of Speyer (1529) failed to produce a long-lasting solution to the "Luther problem," Emperor Charles V sought another opportunity to deal with Luther. He established the Diet of Augsburg for 1530 to take up the religious question again.

Luther was under danger of arrest due to the Edict of Worms, so his colleague Philipp Melanchthon attended. Melanchthon, with Luther's approval, wrote a confession of faith, which was presented to the emperor. It became known as the Augsburg Confession (1530) and was a focused summation of the emerging evangelical or Lutheran faith.

Roman Catholics, as well as the emperor, rejected the confession, leading Melanchthon to compose an apology (defense) of the Augsburg Confession. Since the diet did not settle the religious issues, in early 1531, Lutheran princes banded together in the Schmalkaldic League (from Schmalkalden where their meeting took place). This defensive alliance adopted the Augsburg Confession. By 1537 the League represented thirty-five states and became a powerful force. It lasted another decade until the Schmalkaldic War broke out in 1546. In that year, Martin Luther died. The imperial forces won the Battle of Mühlberg on April 24, 1547. But civil wars continued. In 1548, the Interim of Augsburg was established, granting Protestants the right to have married clergy and celebrate Communion of both kinds (bread and wine). But the Interim was an uneasy "peace."

After more years of fighting, the (second) Diet of Augsburg (1555) sought to end the hostilities. Though many issues remained unsettled, the Peace of Augsburg was finalized on September 25, 1555. It basically provided toleration for Lutheranism by giving each prince the opportunity to choose the faith expression for his territory. The formula was *cuius regio, eius religio*—"he who has the rule determines the religion." Those dissenting could immigrate to another territory. Free cities had to allow both Roman Catholics and Lutherans to practice their faiths.

34 What were the Thirty Years' War and the Peace of Westphalia?

The Thirty Years' War (1618–1648) was a series of conflicts throughout Germany, which became one of Europe's most destructive wars. It began between Roman Catholics and Protestants. It turned into a contest for political power between France and the ruling Habsburg family of Germany.

One hundred years after Luther's Ninety-five Theses, German Protestants celebrated with a jubilee. This offended Roman Catholics. In Bohemia, anti-Protestant violence broke out. When two of the new Roman Catholic King Ferdinand II's counselors who were trying to mediate a dispute were thrown out a castle window, the event was called the Defenestration of Prague. The two men lived. Roman Catholics attributed this to guardian angels. Protestants said it was because the men fell into a pile of manure. But this led Ferdinand (soon to become the Holy Roman Emperor) to attack Protestants.

The war went through varying phases and nearly all the western European nations were drawn into it. Devastation reigned through many areas bringing famine and disease as well as decrease in the populations. Bankruptcy among various nations also occurred.

The war came to a final end with the Peace of Westphalia (1648). In addition to the political changes this brought, the religious settlement was to demand the Peace of Augsburg (1555) be accepted, adding the Reformed, or Calvinist, churches to Roman Catholicism and Lutheranism as recognized religions. The religion of a ruler of a region determined the religion of the particular realm (Lat. *cuius regio, eius religio*). The Peace allowed citizens to emigrate if they could not accept their ruler's religion and also permitted private worship according to one's conscience to be practiced.

The Peace ended the Holy Roman Empire, allowing for a number of autonomous entities. The religious outcomes of the Thirty Years' War provided a different direction for religion in Europe with the recognition of three church bodies and that differing faith expressions could be sanctioned. Many see the Peace as the end of the Protestant "Reformation," even as the Protestant churches that emerged from the Reformation continued with reforms through the years.

35 What was the English Reformation?

Henry Tudor (1491–1547) was a larger-than-life figure who reigned in England as Henry VIII. Today he is remembered for his six wives and their fates: divorced, beheaded, died, divorced, beheaded, survived.

When Henry's marriage to Catherine of Aragon (mother of Mary I, "Bloody Mary," who reigned 1553–1558) did not produce a male heir, Henry sought a divorce to marry Anne Boleyn with whom he had fallen in love. Pope Clement VII refused. So in 1533, Henry secretly married Anne. Henry reenvisioned England as an empire in itself without any earthly superior. Parliament passed acts in 1534: the Succession Act, the Act of Supremacy, and the Treasons Act. These included making the English sovereign the supreme head of the English church. Henry's chief minister, Thomas Cromwell (c. 1485–1540), guided these acts through Parliament and instituted church reforms, influenced by the Lutheran Reformation.

These actions set the stage for what followed in the English Reformation. Under Henry's son, who was only nine years old when he was crowned, King Edward VI (reign 1547–1553), Protestantism advanced. Reformers Martin Bucer and Peter Martyr Vermigli taught at Cambridge, moving the church in a more Reformed direction. Edward's successor, Mary I attempted to restore Roman Catholicism. Nearly three hundred Protestant leaders were martyred, and others fled to Protestant cities on the European continent.

Mary died in 1558 and was succeeded by Henry's daughter with Anne Boleyn, Mary's half-sister, Elizabeth I (reigned 1558–1603). The Elizabethan church in the next half century was led by many Protestant returnees from the continent who became bishops and deans. Theologically, the church moved in a Reformed direction. But rituals and practices from the medieval period continued, and liturgies and worship of the church developed their own forms in the Church of England. A theological "via media" often describes the church's "middle way," trying to establish elements of Protestant reform along with earlier practices. But parties in the church developed: those favoring the established Church of England; those who wanted more liturgical and church reforms—who became known as "Puritans"; and those who believed too much of Roman Catholicism still remained and who separated from the established church. The religious struggles were a main feature of the English Civil War (1642–1651).

36 What was the Elizabethan Settlement?

After the death of Mary Tudor ("Bloody Mary"), her half-sister, the daughter of King Henry VIII and Anne Boleyn, Elizabeth I (1533–1603), became queen. The "Elizabethan Settlement" was

the attempt to resolve religious issues in England and reestablish
the Protestant faith in the land.

Elizabeth was named the "Supreme Governor" of the church
(instead of the previous "Supreme Head") by the Act of Supremacy (1559). This title was to avoid offending Roman Catholics,
who saw the pope as the head of the church, and Protestants, who
saw Christ as the Supreme Head. Under King Edward VI, prior
to Mary Tudor, Protestantism had been developing in England.
Under the Elizabethan Settlement, Edwardian reforms were rein-
troduced and revised. These included the second *Book of Common Prayer* (1552). The Act of Uniformity (1563) introduced the
Thirty-nine Articles of Religion, which were revisions of Thomas
Cranmer's Articles of 1553.

Over Elizabeth's forty-four-year reign (1558–1603), the Church
of England (later, Anglicanism) became the official religion of the
realm. The church underwent a number of changes as it became a
"via media," or "middle way," between Protestant theology of a
Reformed or Calvinist type and liturgical practices that still owed
much to Roman Catholicism. Elizabeth's decisions were made
with advice from her Protestant advisers. But they were met with
mixed results by the "Protestant party" in England. Protestants
were divided into differing groups.

A number of Reformed, or Calvinists, many who were exiles
in Europe under Mary, became known as "Puritans," since they
wanted to purify the church further than the Elizabethan Settlement and eliminate all remnants of Catholicism. This included
the liturgy, clergy vestments over which the Vestments Controversy raged, and saints days. Church of England adherents
supported the various liturgical developments proposed by the
queen and wanted to maintain traditional practices of English
Christianity, in the context of their Protestant and often broadly
Reformed theology. There were also those who felt that even
Puritan suggestions were not radical enough. They did not
conform to the law requiring all to be part of the Church of
England. These nonconformist dissenters were to establish their
own "free churches," and many left England to immigrate to
other lands.

37 Whab was bhe Church of England?

The Elizabethan Settlement (1559) marked Queen Elizabeth's desire to restore the English church to the situation that existed at the end of the reign of her half-brother, Edward VI (1553). This featured a Protestant direction. What became known as Anglicanism became England's official faith expressed through the Church of England, of which the queen was the "Supreme Governor." The term "Anglicanism" did not come into use until the 1830s.

Political and intellectual, as well as theological and ecclesiological (church), influences aided the development of the Church of England in the sixteenth century. These were marked by an emphasis on catholicity and connections with the catholic tradition of the Christian church expressed through the centuries prior to the sixteenth-century Protestant Reformation. This direction began with the English Reformation under King Henry VIII. Under Henry's son, the Protestant King Edward VI, changes to traditional doctrine included the reduction of the seven sacraments to the sacraments of baptism and the Lord's Supper. The second *Book of Common Prayer* (1552) did not express the traditional view of the real presence of Christ in the bread and wine of the Supper.

Under Elizabeth, the Forty-two Articles (issued in 1553), which grew out of Thomas Cranmer's work, were reduced to Thirty-nine Articles (1563) and became the Church of England's doctrinal standard. They are a moderate "midpoint" between Lutheranism and Reformed theology.

Two major justifications of Church of England theology were produced in the Reformation period. John Jewel published his *Apologia ecclesiae Anglicanae* in 1562. The first four volumes of Richard Hooker's *Of the Laws of Ecclesiastical Politie* were published in 1593, the fifth in 1597, and the final three, published after Hooker's death in 1600, appeared in 1648. More than simply a rebuttal of the theology of English Puritans who wanted a church more Reformed in theology, Hooker's work provided a comprehensive defense of the Church of England's theology and church order. His work appealed to Scripture and to reason.

What is called Anglicanism today features an episcopal form of church government, hierarchical in structure. Its three ecclesiastical offices are bishop, priest, and deacon.

38 What was English Puritanism?

Some of those who sought further reforms in the English church during the reign of Elizabeth I (1558–1603) were referred to, initially derisively, as "Precisianists," or "Puritans."

The movement stood in the Reformed theological tradition and was rooted in the work of early English Protestants who were influenced by the Swiss Reformation, such as William Tyndale (c. 1494–1536) and John Hooper (c. 1495–1555). Seeds of the movement emerged in the eight hundred "Marian exiles," those Protestants who left England under the persecution of Queen Mary I (1553–1558), who sought to reintroduce Roman Catholicism into England.

When the Protestant Elizabeth sought to retain clergy vestments (alb, cope, stole, and surplice), the Vestments (Vestiarian) controversy broke out (1560s). Puritans objected that these were what they called popish remnants of Roman Catholicism. These objectors were mostly university-educated clergypersons and some zealous laity, many from Cambridge. They sought an English church reformed after the pattern of Reformed churches on the European continent. Further controversies over the rate and degree of reform ensued.

These conflicts contributed to the English Civil War (1640s) when many Puritans supported the execution of King Charles I (1648). In the aftermath, when Oliver Cromwell was Lord Protector (1653–1658), the period of 1649–1660 featuring republican government has sometimes been called a time of Puritan rule. This period also produced fragmentation. Competing sects emerged. With the restoration of the English monarchy in the reign of Charles II (1660), Puritan political ambitions came to an end when they were purged from the Church of England. Many continued their ministries as "Dissenters" or "Nonconformists," operating outside the state church. They formed Baptist, Congregationalist, and Presbyterian congregations. Toleration was eventually granted with the Toleration Act (1689) under William and Mary.

While early Puritans hoped for structural changes in the church, moderate Puritans such as Richard Greenham (c. 1542–1594), Richard Rogers (c. 1551–1618), and William Perkins (1558–1602) sought pastoral renewal within the national church. Emphases on theology and ethics and a personal spirituality featuring religious disciplines marked the movement. Later Puritans further emphasized self-examination and signs of grace in one's life as expressions of God's election.

39 What was the Scottish Reformation?

Scotland was an independent nation in the sixteenth century. Luther's teachings reached the country in the 1520s and were opposed by the Roman Catholic hierarchy who were able to suppress them.

In 1528, Patrick Hamilton (1504–1528), who had studied at the University of Paris where he imbibed Luther's ideas and tried to introduce them to Scotland, was executed in St. Andrews. George Wishart (c. 1513–1546), whose preaching spread the ideas of the Swiss reformers, was burnt at the stake in 1546. His death enraged supporters, who killed Cardinal David Beaton, the archbishop of St. Andrews, who had ordered Wishart's execution.

Wishart's bodyguard was John Knox (c. 1514–1572), who went on to become the leading Scottish Protestant reformer. Knox published *The First Blast of the Trumpet against the Monstrous Regiment of Women* (1558), which was directed against Queen Mary Guise. At Mary's death (1560), the Scottish Parliament rejected Roman Catholicism, outlawing the Mass, and adopted the Scots Confession (1560), written by Knox and several associates. *The Book of Discipline* established a presbyterian church government, with kirks (local congregations) being governed by elders and joined in local presbyteries, larger units of synods, and a General Assembly of the church.

In 1567, Mary Stuart, Queen of Scots, sanctioned the new Protestant church. But the queen was arrested and imprisoned in June 1567. She was forced to abdicate the throne in July. Mary escaped from Lochleven Castle, where she was held, and fled to England, where she was imprisoned. She was convicted of plotting against Queen Elizabeth and was beheaded in February 1587. Her son, James VI of Scotland, became James I of England and was the king for whom the King James Bible is named.

During James's reign, a moderate episcopacy was introduced. James's son, King Charles I, was committed to this Anglicanism of Archbishop William Laud (1573–1645). But a Scottish movement emerged with a National Covenant (1638), which affirmed the Reformed faith in doctrine, worship, and discipline. All Scots were to sign the covenant. The Covenanters and the English Long Parliament became allied through the Solemn League and Covenant (1643), binding Scotland, England, and Ireland to preserve the Reformed religion of Scotland. Scottish commissioners were sent to the Westminster Assembly (1643–1648), and the Westminster documents became the standards of the Church of Scotland.

40 Who were the Huguenots?

The Huguenots were French Calvinists who as members of the French Reformed Church faced political persecution in the sixteenth century. "Huguenot" may have come from a Swiss term referring to members of the Swiss Confederation, thus "confederates." Or, since the Huguenots often met at night, it may refer to the legend of a night-walking ghost of King Hugo. The term was applied from about 1560.

In 1559, representatives of about fifty churches gathered in Paris to organize the French Reformed Church. A confession of faith, the French Confession, was adopted, along with a form of church discipline. The church's government featured a representative structure of judicatories, which included a consistory (local church), colloquy, provincial synod, and national synod. These are often seen to correspond to presbyterian structures of the local church session, presbytery, synod, and General Assembly.

The church had 2,150 congregations by 1561. But the church faced persecution, leading to the French Wars of Religion (1562–1598). The government-inspired massacre of St. Bartholomew's Day (August 24, 1572) produced Protestant casualties estimated from five thousand to thirty thousand (with twenty thousand often considered a reasonable figure). This atrocity was shocking to Reformed Christians in Europe. Some converted to Catholicism, while others returned to fighting religious wars. Some called for representative government, limiting royal absolutism. The massacre gruesomely displayed the depths of hatred confessional differences brought during this period.

King Henry IV of France brought toleration through the Edict of Nantes (1598), ending the religious wars and guaranteeing civil and religious rights to Huguenots. Later, under Louis XIII and XIV, the Edict was revoked (1685). Thousands of Huguenots were persecuted and forced to accept Catholicism. Over four hundred thousand Huguenots fled throughout Europe and to North America.

The religious persecution of Huguenots through the years produced much suffering and led many to draw on the resources of their Reformed faith.

41 What was the Catholic Reformation?

Movements for reform in the Roman Catholic Church date from the late 1400s to the early 1700s. Historians have used various terms to describe aspects of reform. "Counter Reformation" was used by Protestant historians to describe reforms directly related to Protestantism. "Catholic Reformation" or "Catholic Reform" describes movements not directly related to Protestantism that sought church reforms. "Tridentine Catholicism" designates reforms that emerged after the Council of Trent. "Early Modern Catholicism" refers to emerging Catholicism in its various forms.

Overall, "Catholic Reformation" can refer to ongoing efforts to correct abuses in the church, return the church to its historic heritage as an institution, and evoke a genuine piety in Roman Catholics to be expressed in devotion to the church and its teachings.

In the wake of a great schism in the Roman Catholic Church (1378–1417), new religious orders emerged. Among these were the Capuchins (1520) and the Theatines (1522). The *Devotio Moderna*, founded by the Dutch preacher Geert (Gerhard) Groote (1340–1384), encouraged a life of prayer, penance, and service, embodied in the Brethren of the Common Life movement. Scholars such as Desiderius Erasmus (c. 1466–1536) and Thomas More (1478–1535) were devoted to Scripture study and religious devotion in the church. The Society of Jesus, founded by Ignatius Loyola (1540, Jesuits) was a primary instrument of evangelism and education.

Papal reform by Pope Paul IV (1555–1559) and Pope Pius V (1566–1572) sought to eliminate abuses such as nepotism, to encourage bishops to be pastoral, and to combat heresy. Two expressions were the Papal Inquisition (1542) and the Index of Prohibited Books (1557, revised 1564). The Council of Trent (1545–1563) addressed doctrinal and church life issues.

Throughout, numerous religious orders carried out their vocations and continued to supplement the life of the institutional church with their varying emphases and ministries. Mystical figures and movements, such as Teresa of Ávila (1515–1582) and John of the Cross (1542–1591) sought a deepening of the spiritual life and marked emerging modern Catholicism with impulses that continue today.

42 What was the Colloquy of Poissy?

The last of the large theological debates held between Roman Catholics and Protestants to seek religious reconciliation took place in the village of Poissy, just west of Paris, from September 9 to October 9, 1561. Despite some good will, the colloquy ended in failure, and French Wars of Religion (1562–1598) soon began.

The conference was held by Queen Catherine de Médici (1519–1589), regent for her underage son King Charles IX who, at age eleven, was present. The French Protestants (Huguenots) were represented by Theodore Beza (1519–1605), Calvin's main assistant in Geneva, and Peter Martyr Vermigli (1499–1562), a learned Reformed theologian who had been invited to Oxford by Thomas Cranmer. The Roman Catholics were led by the Cardinal of Lorraine, Charles of Guise (1524–1574), as well as Ignatius Loyola's successor as the General of the Society of Jesus (Jesuits), Diego Laínez (1512–1565).

Beza's opening address presented the Reformed faith. But his comment that the body of Christ in the Lord's Supper was "as far removed from the bread and wine as is heaven from earth" was met with horror by the Roman Catholics, and Beza was accused of blasphemy.

Generally, both sides were hardly disposed toward reconciliation. Lorraine asked Beza to affirm the teachings on the Lord's Supper found in the Lutheran Augsburg Confession (1530) as a condition for the conference continuing. Lorraine's act has been seen either as an act of bad faith—to discredit the Protestants by showing that they could not agree among themselves—or perhaps as an attempt at mediation since it would mean that the Reformed were not being asked directly to endorse a Roman Catholic tenet of theology. Beza declared the request was inappropriate, and the Reformed did not sign the Confession.

A smaller form of the colloquy continued, but no satisfactory formulations succeeded in bringing the two sides together. In the aftermath, the French Wars of Religion began in 1562 and thousands died.

Theology

4

Theological Expressions

43 What was Scholasticism?

In the medieval period, the theology of the schools (Lat. *scholae*) was called "scholasticism." After the capture of Jerusalem by Islamic invaders (638) until its recapture in the Christian crusades (1099), Christian theology was largely the work of monks who studied the Scriptures, the early Christian theologians, and classical literature as part of their calling and devotion.

Anselm of Canterbury (1033–1109) taught that theology began in faith and led to further understanding. This had also been the method of the great early theologian St. Augustine (354–430). But balances between faith and reason were difficult to maintain.

Peter Abelard (1079–1142) and his student, Peter Lombard (c. 1100–1160) applied the tools of reason to divine revelation. Lombard used this method and wrote what became the standard textbook on theology for four centuries. Thomas Aquinas (1224 or 1225–1274) produced his *Summa theologica*, through 24 volumes, 631 questions, and 10,000 objections. Aquinas believed reason and revelation are compatible. God's grace does not destroy nature; it perfects it.

Scholasticism stressed human rationality and the use of reason (though admitting that some Christian doctrines transcended reason). Renaissance humanists such as Desiderius Erasmus and Lorenzo Valla were critical of scholastic method.

Luther and Calvin criticized medieval scholastic theology for regarding human reason too highly and relying too much on Aristotle. The emphasis of Protestant Reformers on Scripture—received in faith—as the source for faith and theological understanding put theology on a different basis from medieval scholasticism.

Scholastic method was used by second-generation Protestant theologians—both Lutheran and Reformed—to systematize and organize insights from earlier reformers. This led to the seventeenth-century era being characterized as a period of post-Reformation Protestant scholasticism. The emphasis was on careful analysis of biblical texts as well as the use of reason to derive further theological insights.

44 What was Renaissance Humanism?

The period of the Renaissance, beginning in the fourteenth century, was marked by a rebirth of learning and new directions for education. During this period in Europe, "humanism" emerged as a method of learning focused on rediscovering and recovering literary sources from classical antiquity—Roman and Greek, as well as Christian. The humanist motto was: *Ad fontes!* "To the sources!"

The humanist movement emphasized studies related to the life of the world, what we today would call the humanities, rather than the speculative issues that marked the content of much medieval education. Humanists emphasized rhetoric, or the art of persuasion, rather than dialectic, the art of logic, or abstract reasoning associated with scholasticism—the methods of the schools.

The focus of humanists on recovering the literature of the ancient world and interpreting it with an eye toward its meaning for life was important for Protestant Reformers. The most famous humanist scholar was Desiderius Erasmus (1467–1536). Erasmus produced editions of classical texts, including the Greek New Testament (1516). The humanist emphasis was on study of original source documents, interpreted in their linguistic and social contexts. Reformers such as Huldrych Zwingli and John Calvin were trained as humanists and brought the tools of this approach to learning to their theological studies and emphases.

Humanism was an important background influence on Protestant Reformers. Many humanists were critical of the Roman Catholic Church for its speculative, scholastic theology. But while humanism provided tools for Protestant scholars to approach texts—especially the Bible—the Renaissance humanist movement itself did not adopt the theological understandings that marked the Protestant Reformation. Erasmus collided with Luther over the question of free will and differed over the nature of God's grace. Over time, a clear divergence developed between humanists who remained in the Roman Catholic Church and those who adopted Protestantism.

45 What were indulgences?

The immediate trigger for Luther and the beginning of the Reformation was the selling of indulgences by Johann Tetzel in 1516 and 1517. Tetzel (c. 1465–1519) was a Dominican priest, touring European cities selling indulgences to raise money for construction of what became St. Peter's basilica in Rome. A famous slogan associated with this indulgence was "When a coin in the coffer rings, a soul from purgatory springs."

In medieval Roman Catholic theology, purgatory was the place where souls of the faithful dead experienced painful purification and cleansing from sin before they could enter heaven. In the church, "indulgences" could be issued on behalf of the departed as a pardon for the temporal punishments that remained for them after repentance and forgiveness of sins by a priest. Friends and relatives of the deceased could pay to have part of the deceased's "debt" decreased and thus reduce the time spent in purgatory. The church began to use revenues from indulgences to fund building projects.

Luther protested the doctrine of indulgences and made his views known to the Archbishop of Mainz and Magdeburg. This led to Luther's issuing his Ninety-five Theses, traditionally said to have been posted on the church door in Wittenberg on the eve of All Saints' Day, on October 31, 1517. These were theological propositions Luther proposed for academic debate, an established practice.

Among other things, Luther's theses challenged the church's claims for indulgences and also raised the question of the values of indulgences at all. He questioned the power of the pope to extend the power of indulgences to souls in purgatory. Theologically, Luther was questioning how salvation is given by a righteous God. Ecclesiastically, Luther was questioning the jurisdiction of the pope. These two dimensions continued throughout Luther's conflict with Rome as theological disputes were coupled with clashes over the nature of the church.

46 What were Luther's Ninety-five Theses?

Luther's Ninety-five Theses were the opening act in the drama of Luther and the Roman Catholic Church. When he posted these ninety-five propositions for academic discussion on October 31, 1517, Luther assumed that the issues he was raising as a theology professor would be debated and where he could show that the church had erred in its teachings, changes would be made. But this was not to be.

While Luther's initial concern was with indulgences, the Ninety-five Theses ranged over other areas. These went beyond the critiques of clergy shortcomings or practical abuses raised by others. For Luther, the eternal salvation of God's people was at stake because the church had not rightly presented the true teachings of the Christian gospel. This set a major confrontation in motion.

Among the topics that Luther's theses touched on were sin and salvation. Instead of the church's formal penitential process where priests prescribed acts of satisfaction, Luther believed sin and its consequences must be dealt with throughout life as one's relationship with God is formed (thesis 1). Throughout the theses, Luther questioned and challenged the penitential system, saying the church's focus should be on faith and repentance. It is not a "treasury of merits" that the church possesses in order to pay for the release of souls from purgatory. Instead, the church's true treasure is "the Most Holy Gospel of the glory of God" (thesis 62). Christians must follow Christ, their head (thesis 94).

Luther's theses were written in Latin. Some of his students translated them into German and had them printed. They became a bestseller and were translated into most other European languages. Luther became a "celebrity."

Pope Leo X was not pleased. Theological debates followed at Leipzig and Augsburg. The pope excommunicated Luther. Luther developed his theological understandings based on Holy Scripture. His Ninety-five Theses led to many other writings where he explained his understanding of the Christian gospel. The Ninety-five Theses are often considered to mark the beginning of the Protestant Reformation, which has permanently affected the Christian church.

47 What was the Augsburg Confession?

The Augsburg Confession is the major Lutheran statement of faith (1530, Lat. *Confessio Augustana*), which became the primary confession of Lutheran churches. An "Altered" Augsburg Confession (*Confessio Augustana variata*) was published by Philipp Melanchthon (1540). It contained an article 10 on the Lord's Supper, which could be read as a change from Luther's position on the presence of Christ in the Supper.

The final version of the 1530 Augsburg Confession was written by Melanchthon in preparation for the Diet of Augsburg. Emperor Charles V demanded the Wittenberg theologians present a statement of faith to affirm the emerging Protestant theology. On June 25, 1530, Melanchthon presented a Latin and German edition of the confession to the emperor.

The confession was intended to distinguish Luther and Melanchthon's views from those of Huldrych Zwingli and others in regard to the Lord's Supper. It was also to mark the differences between their views and those of the emerging Anabaptist movements. Positively, Melanchthon wanted to show the confession was in continuity with the theology of the early church while also being differentiated from Roman Catholic theology.

The confession was composed of twenty-eight articles in two parts. Articles 1 through 21 focused on the "Chief Articles of the Faith." Here main doctrines such as original sin, justification, church and sacraments, and free will and good works were covered. The final seven articles considered the abuses that needed remedied in the church. These were Communion with both bread and wine, clerical celibacy, the Mass, confession of sins to a priests, monastic vows, and ecclesiastical power.

While the Augsburg Confession bolstered the faith of Lutherans, it did not achieve a doctrinal consensus with Roman Catholics. Leading Catholic theologians published a Confutation of the Augsburg Confession (1530) to which Melanchthon responded with his Apology of the Augsburg Confession (1531).

Melanchthon's altering of article 10 sought common ground among conflicting theological parties. John Calvin was able to sign the altered confession (1541). But the original confession came to be considered the more preferred confessional standard.

48 What was the *Book of Concord*?

On the fiftieth anniversary of the Augsburg Confession, the *Book of Concord* (also *Concordia*) was published on June 25, 1580. This book was adopted as the definitive collection of Lutheran confessions as well as authoritative for Lutheran preaching, teaching, and polity (church government).

The *Book of Concord* was occasioned by the ratification of the Formula of Concord (1577), a confession designed to foster theological unity in Lutheranism in the years after the deaths of Luther (d. 1546) and Melanchthon (d. 1560). The Formula set forth the acceptable range of theological views for Lutheran churches. It treats topics under twelve headings. Its two parts were the "Solid Declaration" and the "Epitome" (summary).

The *Book of Concord* is composed of ten documents. There are three ancient ecumenical standards: the Apostles', Nicene, and

Athanasian creeds. Documents from the Reformation era are the Augsburg Confession (1530) and the Apology of the Augsburg Confession (1531), the Smalcald (also Schmalkaldic) Articles (1537), Luther's "Treatise on the Power and Primacy of the Pope" (1537), Luther's Small Catechism (1529) and Large Catechism (1529), as well as the Formula of Concord (1577).

The work of second-generation Lutheran reformers, Martin Chemnitz (1522–1586) and Jakob Andreae (1528–1590) over a number of years sought to build consensus and support for the *Book of Concord*. The work brought an end to inter-Lutheran conflicts between Lutheran groups that spread over thirty years. "Gnesio [genuine] Lutherans" saw themselves as the true followers of Luther, instead of Melanchthon. "Philippists" were followers of Melanchthon, often accused of being "crypto-Calvinists," as holding Calvinist opinions and too ready to compromise with Roman Catholicism. The *Book of Concord* features works by both Luther and Melanchthon. The acceptance of the book was a decisive moment in a period of confessionalism, when Europe's territories were delineated by their confessions: Lutheran, Reformed, and Roman Catholic.

49 What were Zwingli's Sixty-seven Articles?

The sixty-seven theological articles by Huldrych Zwingli were presented to the city council of Zurich on January 29, 1523. These were Articles for a Disputation in which Zwingli would vindicate his understanding of the Christian gospel against charges of heresy. The result would determine whether Zurich would remain Roman Catholic or adopt the reforms Zwingli as the lead minister of the city was promoting.

Some six hundred people attended the presentation of the articles. In the audience were representatives from Rome as well as the Bishop of Constance who had oversight of Zurich. Zwingli presented the articles, and the City Council supported them. The council gave Zwingli the right to preach from the Bible and to carry out Protestant reforms. It withdrew the canton from the jurisdiction of the Roman Catholic bishop and affirmed the ban against preaching and teaching that was not based on the Bible. By these actions, the Zurich Council officially adopted the Reformation, led by Zwingli.

Zwingli said his preaching and the articles were based on the Scripture. The Scriptures were considered inspired by God" (Gk. *theopneustos*; cf. 2 Tim. 3:16). He said he was willing to be instructed and corrected but only from the Scriptures and not from other sources.

Among the Sixty-seven Articles are:

- Jesus Christ redeemed us and reconciled us to God and is the only way to salvation.
- Works of penance do not remit sins, only Christ.
- Our salvation is based on faith in the gospel; our damnation on unbelief.
- All who live in Christ are Christ's members and children of God, joined in fellowship as the church.
- All Christians should do their utmost to see that the gospel of Christ is preached.
- Christians should reject the pope, the Mass, purgatory, and the intercession of the saints.
- God alone, not priests, forgives sins.
- All Christians are free to eat all foods at any time.
- Temporal power is established by God.

These Sixty-seven Articles are less famous but more comprehensive than Luther's Ninety-five Theses. They are formative in marking the beginning of the Swiss Reformation.

50 What were the Schleitheim Articles?

The Schleitheim Articles were originally called *The Brotherly Union of a Number of Children of God concerning Seven Articles.* They were adopted on February 24, 1527, and were probably written by Michael Sattler (c. 1490–1527), a former monk. The articles are regarded as the first Anabaptist statement of faith. They were named for the town of Schleitheim, Switzerland, on the Swiss-German border and attempted to bring unity to Swiss-Austrian-

South German Anabaptists who had broken into various groups since they began in Zurich two years before.

The seven articles are concise, and they are a manifesto for the emerging concerns of the Anabaptist movement.

1. Baptism is for all who believe they are forgiven by faith in Jesus Christ and who have repented of sin. Infant baptism is explicitly forbidden.
2. The community of the baptized will ban those who have broken baptismal promises and lapsed from newness of life in Christ. This keeps the community pure.
3. Participants in the Lord's Supper, which is a remembrance of Christ's broken body and shed blood, can be only those who have been baptized.
4. Separation from the world prescribes believers to maintain a separation between themselves and unbelievers in the surrounding world. This represents a dualism between the Christian community and secular culture.
5. Guidelines for pastors discuss calling pastors to church communities, duties of the pastoral office, and church discipline of a pastor. Pastors are to be of good repute to silence unbelievers.
6. Secular government concerns the "sword," which is ordained by God but apart from "the perfection of Christ," and is the instrument to bring punishment to the wicked. In the Christian community, only the ban is to be used for discipline. No Christian believers may bear the sword, sit in judgment on others, or serve in secular governments.
7. Forbidding of oaths is to follow Christ's command. In secular contexts where oaths were required, Anabaptists were perceived as threatening societal order.

51 What was Calvin's *Institutes of the Christian Religion*?

John Calvin's *Institutes of the Christian Religion* was Calvin's greatest theological work in which he dealt with major topics and themes of Scripture. The *Institutes* was to instruct persons in the Christian faith. The *Institutes* supplemented the commentaries on most of the books of the Bible that Calvin wrote over time as well as the preaching Calvin did multiple times per week. Calvin did not want his commentaries to go deeply into formal theological matters, so the emphasis could stay with the biblical texts. So his *Institutes* emerged out of Calvin's ongoing interpretation of Scripture. Calvin gathered up his biblical insights into a more systematic form in the *Institutes* to provide an overall framework for interpreting the Bible.

Through the years, Calvin published new editions of the *Institutes*. The book grew from six to eighty chapters from 1536–1560. When Calvin wrote a new edition of the *Institutes* in Latin, the language of theological discourse, he followed it up with a new edition in French so that persons could read it in their vernacular. The book was initially addressed to the French king, Francis I, and sought to gain a better hearing for Protestants at the French court. This address remained the same throughout the editions. Calvin's final Latin edition was published in 1559, followed by a French edition in 1560.

After Calvin's first edition of the *Institutes,* the work was divided into four books: (1) "The Knowledge of God the Creator"; (2) "The Knowledge of God the Redeemer in Christ"; (3) "The Way in Which We Receive the Grace of Christ: What Benefits Come to Us from It, and What Effects Follow"; and (4) "The External Means or Aids by Which God Invites Us into the Society of Christ and Holds Us There." Broadly, these correspond to focuses on God, Jesus Christ, the Holy Spirit, and the church.

The *Institutes* has been translated into a number of languages. It presents an ordered discussion of the Christian faith in a way that Luther did not provide. The book is a classic expression of the Reformed faith.

52 What was the Geneva Bible?

The Geneva Bible was a translation of the Bible into English by Marian exiles, Protestants who left England when the Roman Catholic Mary Tudor became queen (reigned 1553–1558). This

Bible was important to English Protestants for its translation and its textual notes, which conveyed emerging Reformed theology that was highly influenced by John Calvin.

The translation, carried out in Geneva, was based on the work of William Whittingham, who had published his New Testament translation in 1557. The Geneva Bible extended this work, while Whittingham collaborated with Anthony Gilby and was assisted by Thomas Sampson, Christopher Goodman, and possibly others. The complete Geneva Bible was published on May 10, 1560.

The Geneva Bible featured various reading aids, including prefaces, maps, diagrams, and extensive marginal notes expressing theological perspectives. The "Argument" of each biblical book was presented along with summaries of individual chapters. Together these features conveyed Reformed theology and made the Scriptures more accessible to individual readers. It was the first Bible to use verse numbers.

The Geneva Bible was not well-received in England by Queen Elizabeth who saw it as a way of accelerating changes in the church advocated by Puritan leaders. But the response of the English people was quite different. The Geneva Bible was produced in small formats, unlike the large folio officially sanctioned "Great Bible" (1539), which was chained in churches. It was affordable and sold in great numbers. The first edition published in England was in 1576, and some 140 editions were published in England until 1644. The Geneva Bible was also very influential in Scotland. Overall, it was one of the most important Bibles in English-printing history.

A revised New Testament translation and more extensive marginal notes were produced by the Puritan scholar Laurence Tomson in 1587. This enhanced the "study Bible" dimensions of the book. In 1599, annotations on the book of Revelation by Franciscus Junius replaced Tomson's notes.

The Geneva Bible provided a scholarly base for future English Bible translations, notably the King James Bible (1611). Through all its features, the Geneva Bible enabled English readers to have a vernacular translation and guided their theological understandings in Reformed directions.

53 What was the King James Bible?

The King James Bible (1611) was authorized in England by King James VI of Scotland, who became King James I of England (1566–1625; reign 1603–1625), son of Mary Queen of Scots, at the Hampton Court Conference (1604). It grew into being a cherished part of English literature and the Bible of millions of Christians, who became familiar with its classic language and translations.

At Hampton Court, King James assented to the request of the Puritan John Rainolds (1549–1607; also "Reynolds") that a new English translation of the Bible be prepared. Rainolds claimed that earlier official versions from the times of King Henry VIII and King Edward VI were corrupt. The king appointed a translation committee of fifty-four scholars who were also devoted Christians and well suited for this work (forty-seven actually worked on the translation, including Rainolds). Only one member was not a clergyperson. Six subcommittees met in the cities of Cambridge, Oxford, and Westminster. In the preface, the translators explained their doctrinal and linguistic principles. In part, the King James Bible was a response to the Roman Catholic Rheims-Douay translation (New Testament, 1582; complete Bible, 1610).

The "King James Version" (KJV) or "Authorized Version" (AV, later) did not use marginal notes for doctrinal descriptions, like the Geneva Bible (1560). Theologically, the scholars believed that persons can understand the Word of God without these glosses. Politically, the king indicated that some of the marginal notes in the Geneva were offensive because they promoted civil disobedience. The king wanted the translation to be consistent with the understanding of the church (ecclesiology) held by the Church of England, especially in its episcopal structure. The Bishops' Bible (1568; revised 1602) was to be a primary guide for the translators, though other earlier English Bibles, including the Geneva Bible, could be used. The translators began work in 1604. A complete folio Bible was published by the king's printer in 1611. The first edition published in Scotland was in 1633.

The King James Bible has been recognized as one of the—or *the*—most important book in English literature and culture. It contributed over 250 idioms to the English language. Contemporary English translations use manuscripts unknown to the seventeenth-century translators; so a number of verses in today's translations show pronounced differences from the KJV.

54 What were the Thirty-nine Articles?

Also known as the Articles of Religion, the Thirty-nine Articles (1563) were derived from the Forty-two Articles (issued in 1553) and came to serve as the doctrinal standard of the Church of England.

During the reign of King Edward VI, the Forty-two Articles were written under the auspices of Thomas Cranmer, Archbishop of Canterbury, to provide a standard of belief for the Protestant church established under King Henry VIII. Under Queen Elizabeth, the Forty-two Articles were revised and reduced to Thirty-nine.

The Thirty-nine Articles are not in the form of a systematic theology as much as an occasion to discuss matters of controversy that were of contemporary significance. The Articles had developed over time with various political and religious influences at work through the years. Thus, they did not try to develop a formal or more "complete" theology. These factors led to the Articles being interpreted in various ways, perhaps an intention of their authors. Basically the Articles seek to define the church's views against Roman Catholic corruptions and doctrines; and in relation to Lutheran, Reformed, and Anabaptist theologies.

Articles 1 through 5 deal with the Trinity, incarnation, atonement, and the resurrection. Articles 6 through 8 name the sources of Christian belief: Scripture and the three ancient creeds (Apostles', Nicene, Athanasian). Articles 9 through 18 are on the doctrine of humanity and the spiritual state of saved yet sinful persons. Articles 19 through 21, 23, and 36 discuss the church's constitution, order, and authority. Article 22 opposes the "Romish doctrine" of purgatory. Article 24 insists on prayers and services in the vernacular (opposed to the Latin used by Roman Catholics). Articles 25 through 31 present the doctrine of the sacraments. Articles on the clergy, excommunication, and so on follow in 32 through 35. Finally, articles 37 through 39 consider the church and Christians themselves in relation to the state and private property.

Today, clergy of the Church of England have only to acknowledge the Thirty-nine Articles as one of the church's historical descriptions of Christian faith and that they witness to the faith revealed in Scripture and expressed in the early church's Apostles' and Nicene creeds.

55 What was the Synod of Dort?

Jacob (James) Arminius (1560–1609) studied theology under Theodore Beza in Geneva. But Arminius became critical of the doctrines of predestination, free will, and grace as taught by Calvin and further by Beza. Arminius taught at the University of Leiden where from 1604 he debated with colleague Franciscus Gomarus (1563–1641). Arminius argued that human free will could respond to God's grace and through repentance attain salvation. He claimed that God's saving grace could be resisted and believers could lose their salvation. It was God's foreknowledge, rather than election and predestination, that saw who would or would not believe and attain salvation.

After his death, the "Arminians" (also called "Remonstrants") formulated their views in a "Remonstrance," five theological propositions. To settle the controversy, the Reformed Church in the United Provinces of the Netherlands held a Synod at Dordrecht (November 13, 1618, through May 29, 1619; Synod of Dort) with participation from other European Reformed churches.

The Synod rejected the Remonstrance, condemned the Remonstrants as heretics, and dismissed two hundred ministers. It established central tenets of Calvinism, often expressed by the acronym TULIP:

- *T*otal depravity means humanity is lost in sin with no ability to respond to Christ in faith and receive salvation.
- *U*nconditional election is God's free choice of those who will be saved ("elect"), receive grace and the gift of faith, without consideration of foreseen faith or human merit.
- *L*imited atonement means Christ's atonement is not intended for everyone but is for and benefits only God's elect.
- *I*rresistible grace indicates God's grace for salvation cannot be resisted by the elect.
- *P*erseverance of the saints maintains the elect will be continue to eternal life and will not fall away from grace.

These theological tenets are sometimes called "The Five Points of Calvinism." The synod did not teach the view of some (including Gomarus) that God had predestined the fall of Adam and Eve into sin (supralapsarianism).

56 What was the Westminster Confession of Faith?

The Westminster Confession was part of the Westminster Standards—documents produced by the Westminster Assembly, which actively met at Westminster Abbey in London from 1643 to 1648. The Assembly of 121 "divines" (clergy) was charged by the Long ("Puritan") Parliament to reform the Church of England. It functioned as an advisory group when Parliament was in an open struggle with King Charles I.

The Assembly met during the English Civil War and produced a Confession of Faith (1647), instead of merely revising the church's Thirty-nine Articles. The Assembly also wrote a Larger and Shorter Catechism, a Directory for Public Worship, and a Form of Church Government.

Due to political events, the Westminster Confession was never adopted by the English church but became the major doctrinal standard of the Church of Scotland (Presbyterian). It has also been a continuing confessional standard of American Presbyterianism and other English-speaking Reformed churches.

The Confession is marked by a strong article on Holy Scripture as the revealed Word of God. Scripture is inspired by God and is to be "the rule of faith and life." The Confession stresses the sovereignty of God and God's "eternal decree" (purpose), which ordains all that comes to pass. God's providence is God's involvement in and guidance of history and the created order, as well in the life of the church and all Christians. The Confession unites God's covenant with God's election of those who will be saved, conveying how God's election works in the history of God's people (church) and their actions in response to God. It also details the Christian life, the sanctification or growth of the Christian in holiness as adopted children of God who will ultimately be glorified in heaven. God's law instructs Christians to obey God's will. The purpose of Christian life is the glory of God, who alone is "Lord of the conscience."

57 What were major catechisms in the Reformation era?

Catechisms (from Greek *kat chein*; "to instruct") go back to the time of early Christianity and were devised to teach the young in the basics of Christian faith. By the Middle Ages, catechisms were printed summaries used for education. Movable type enabled catechisms to become an important form of religious literature.

Luther produced two major catechisms, which became part of the *Book of Concord*, the Lutheran doctrinal standard. His Large Catechism (1528–1529) was to assist clergy in giving instruction in the faith. His Small Catechism (1529) was built around the Ten Commandments Apostles' Creed, Lord's Prayer, and Sacraments.

The Anabaptist *Tablet of Christian Teaching* (1527), by Balthasar Hubmaier, was divided into two parts. The first focuses on the ordinance of baptism and the second on the ordinance of the Lord's Supper.

Among many catechisms of the Reformed tradition, Calvin's two Geneva Catechisms of 1537/1538 (French, 1537; Latin, 1538) and 1542/1545 (French, 1542; Latin, 1545) guided the Genevan church. The Heidelberg Catechism (1563) represented a moderate Reformed faith, appealing to the mind and heart, and was one of the most widely used Reformed standards. The Shorter and Larger Catechisms of the Westminster Assembly (1648), for laity and for pastors, have been very influential.

The first catechism of the Church of England appeared in the *Book of Common Prayer* (1549) and was later expanded (1559) to include a "Catechism for Children." This was a minimalist catechism, barely doing more than setting forth the Apostles' Creed, Ten Commandments, and Lord's Prayer. Larger catechisms soon appeared, including Alexander Nowell's, *A Catechisme, or First Instruction and Learning of Christian Religion* (1570).

Roman Catholic catechisms were stimulated during the Reformation period. Erasmus wrote a couple (1514, 1533), seeking to rejuvenate educational reform and the ancient catechumenateor people being instructed by catechisms. Georg Witzel's (1501–1573) *Instuctio puerorum Ecclesiae* (1542; *Instruction of the Young of the Church*) featured a salvation-history approach through telling the Christian story. Most popular was the Jesuit Peter Canisius' (1521–1597), *Parvus catechismus catholicorum* (1559; *Small Catholic Catechism*) with its question-and-answer form.

Through the period as doctrinal lines rigidified, catechetical emphases shifted from instruction in basic Christian teaching to strengthening convictions for particular church theologies.

5

Theological Topics
of Christian Faith

58 **What were the *solas* of the Reformation?**

Sometimes the Protestant Reformation is described by its distinctive emphases, using the Latin term *sola* (*solus, soli*), meaning "alone." These highlight what Protestants found as core theological convictions.

Sola gratia (grace alone). God's grace is the unmerited favor God gives. It is God's free act of salvation and forgiveness given to sinful humans in Jesus Christ. It is not earned or deserved. As Paul put it, "For by grace you have been saved through faith, and this is not your own doing; it is the gift of God—not the result of works, so that no one may boast" (Eph. 2:8–9).

Sola fide (faith alone). Sinners receive God's grace by faith. Faith is belief, trust, and obedience to God as revealed in Jesus Christ. Faith is the means by which we know Jesus Christ and receive the gift of salvation by believing in him (John 6:40); "the one who is righteous will live by faith" (Gal. 3:11).

Sola Christo (Christ alone). Jesus Christ is the only one through whom salvation can be received. Christ is fully human and fully God and the "one mediator between God and humankind" (1 Tim. 2:5). Christ's death on the cross brings forgiveness of sin and his resurrection secure eternal life for all who believe in him (John 3:16).

Sola Scriptura (Scripture alone). God has revealed God's self through Scripture, the Word of God. Scripture is the authority for Christian belief and Christian living. The Protestant Reformers rejected the Roman Catholic view that authority for the church comes through Scripture plus the traditions and teachings of the Roman church. The Bible is the means through which Jesus Christ is revealed and becomes known to us.

Soli Deo gloria (To the glory of God alone). The Reformers emphasized that all Christian life and activity is to be carried out not to bring glory to one's self, but to bring glory to God. Paul's command directs: "Whatever you do, do everything for the glory of God" (1 Cor. 10:31).

59 What is the authority of Scripture?

The issue of authority is central for Christian faith and for Christian churches. What is the proper source for what we believe and what we do? This is a key question for all churches and for individual Christians.

Protestant churches in the Reformation all agreed that there is no authority greater than the authority of Holy Scripture as the source and guide for churches and Christian believers. This was a point of strong contention raised by Luther against the Roman church. Like other Protestants who came after him, Luther contended it is Scripture and Scripture alone (*sola Scriptura*) that is the foundation of authority for the church. Other sources of authority—such as church tradition, reason, or the promptings of the Holy Spirit must be only secondary. Scripture is the place where God's Word and God's will is expressed. As the church interprets Scripture through the work of the Holy Spirit, God is revealed and communicates with God's people. God's word in Scripture reforms the church's life and teachings.

Scripture is the revelation of God. Reformation churches agreed that Scripture is inspired by God (2 Tim. 3:16). The way inspiration works is a mystery. But the churches believe God worked through human writers who, by the inspiration of the Holy Spirit, conveyed what God wanted to be communicated. In Scripture, God's divine message is expressed in human words.

The message conveyed in Scripture is the message of God's salvation in Jesus Christ. Scripture's purpose is theological: to provide all things necessary for salvation. Holy Scripture is the only place where this revelation of God can be found. It is the only source for the most important message in history: God's love in Jesus Christ (cf. John 3:16; Rom. 5:8).

Protestants have maintained the inseparability of Word and Spirit. The Word of God in Scripture is authenticated and "comes alive" by the work of the Holy Spirit. The Holy Spirit of God witnesses or testifies to the Scriptures as God's Word, and the Spirit enables us to interpret Scripture in the ongoing life of the church. Word and Spirit are inextricably bound up together.

60 What is the Trinity?

Protestant churches in the time of the Reformation received and accepted the doctrine of the Trinity from the ancient church and through medieval Catholicism. It took the early church many years to find a suitable way to express its view of God. Church councils at Nicaea (325) and Constantinople (381) affirmed that Christians believe in and worship one God in three persons. God is One God, as the Jews believed in the Old Testament (Deut. 6:4); and God is three persons: Father, Son, and Holy Spirit, to which the New Testament witnesses. God is one in substance and three eternal Persons.

The three Persons are of the same "substance"—Godness. They are all equal in power and glory. They are all to be worshiped. As the hymn puts it: "God in three persons, blessed Trinity!" In this Trinitarian faith, Reformation churches agreed with the ancient councils, as well as Roman Catholic and Orthodox churches.

Christian churches in the Western tradition affirm that the Holy Spirit "proceeds from the Father and the Son" (Nicene Creed). Churches in the Eastern tradition (Eastern Orthodoxy) affirm the Spirit "proceeds from the Father." This difference split Christian churches into the Western and Eastern branches in 1054.

Within Protestantism, the Reformed tradition has been marked by an emphasis on God's sovereignty—God is Lord of the universe. This includes human history where, according to the doctrine of providence, God's will is being carried out in governing and guiding history, including our human lives.

The Lutheran tradition, following Luther, also emphasizes God's "hiddenness" in the world. That is, God's power and saving purposes in Jesus Christ is not obvious or knowable from the world or from human reason. Instead, we find God in the most unlikely place: in the human Christ. Jesus, humiliated in his death on the cross, is where we find God—by faith, given by the Holy Spirit.

61 Who is Jesus Christ?

Like the doctrine of the Trinity, the doctrine of Jesus Christ (Christology) was not a contended doctrine at the time of the Reformation. The Protestant Reformers accepted the teachings of ancient church councils in their formulations of who Jesus Christ is.

The Christian church has believed that Jesus Christ, the second Person of the Trinity, became a human being in his incarnation: "The Word became flesh and lived among us" (John 1:14). Jesus was fully human, taking on a complete human nature in his incarnation. Jesus was fully human but also fully divine. He had two natures (human and divine) in one Person.

In the early church, some theologians had emphasized one of the natures of Christ at the expense of the other. But the church knew both the human and the divine natures of Christ must be fully present in Jesus Christ. They are united in the one Person even as each dimension is expressed. In the Gospels, we see instances of Jesus' divine power, in his miracles, for example (Luke 8:40–56), as well as his very human emotions, in weeping at the death of his friend Lazarus (John 11:35).

Theologically, the Reformers taught that belief in Jesus as one Person with two natures was crucial for his work in bringing salvation, especially through his death on the cross. If Jesus were not fully divine, his death would have no power to save sinful humans. His death would be like the death of all other persons who had

gone before him. If Jesus were not fully human, he could not have
identified completely with humans and taken on himself in his
death, the sins that humans need to have forgiven (see Heb. 4:15).
For salvation to occur, the mediator, the savior, the one who died
for us must be one person with a divine and human nature—Jesus
Christ himself.

62 What is the human condition?

All Christians believe God created humanity "good," in a relationship of love and trust in its creator (Gen. 1). But sin entered
the picture (Gen. 3) and now the human condition has changed.
Protestant Reformers disagreed on issues relating to human nature
and salvation.

On the issue of original sin, Protestants agreed with Roman
Catholic theology. Both traditions were influenced by the teachings of Augustine (354–430). In the ancient church, Augustine's
views about the nature and extent of sin were important. They
were picked up by medieval Roman Catholic theologians, even
as there were differing paths of interpretation. What was con-
stant, however, was Augustine's view that humanity was completely fallen—separated from loving and trusting God—because
of human sin. The biblical accounts of the "fall" of Adam and Eve
in the garden of Eden (Gen. 3) were interpreted as showing the
rupture of this relationship, later described in dire terms by the
apostle Paul who taught that "all have sinned and fall short of
the glory of God" (Rom. 3:23). The result is that "the wages of sin
is death" (6:23).

"Original sin" refers to sin being associated with the "origins"
of the human race. The church has taught that sin is inherited, in
the sense that it is the condition of all humans by virtue of our "first
parents"—whoever they may have been. No one can escape original sin. It is a loss of relationship with God that becomes expressed
as humans break God's laws, fall short of God's desires for how to
live, and rebel against God's will for our lives.

The Reformers understood original sin as causing a complete

break in the divine/human relationship. Sin affects the fullness and totality of our lives. Human reason is affected so that humans use their minds to rebel against God. Human reasoning cannot bring one to a true knowledge of God—only Scripture as God's divine revelation can do that. So also, human freedom to do the "good"—God's will—is impaired as well. This was to become a contested issue by the Reformers with the Roman Catholics and also a debated issue among the Reformers themselves.

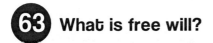 What is free will?

The issue of "free will"—the ability of humans to "want" to do something, to be able to "choose" what to do was a debated issue by the time of the Reformation. In the Roman Catholic tradition, Thomas Aquinas (1224 or 1225–1274) contended humans have the free choice to choose one object or one course of action instead of another. Medieval theologians interpreted this to mean that humans have the free will to move toward God and establish merit that can lead to justification or salvation.

In the mid-1520s, Erasmus and Luther debated this issue. In 1518, Luther (following Augustine) denied humans have free will because of the power of human (original) sin. Erasmus's *Discourse on Free Will* (*De libero arbitrio diatribe*, 1524) claimed that the human will has the power to decide whether or not it will turn toward eternal salvation. Faith formed by love (good works) can bring salvation.

Luther responded with *On the Bondage of the Will* (*De servo arbitrio*, 1525), where he claimed the damage done to humanity by original sin means human reason as well the human will are affected by sin to the degree that humans cannot "will" or "choose" to move toward God. Only the power of God's grace can bring salvation. This was also the view of John Calvin.

Luther's view did not mean people are "puppets" and cannot make everyday life decisions—like whether or not to pick up an object. These are matters "below"—matters not involving salvation. But because of sin, humans cannot "will the good."

Sinful humans will always choose sin or evil instead of choosing to receive salvation. Human actions are not forced; they are free expressions of one's will. So people are responsible for their actions. But sinful people have sinful wills and thus do not have the "free will" to accept the gospel of Christ. Only God, through the work of the Holy Spirit, can bring salvation and release from the power of sin and death.

Luther's and Calvin's views emphasize salvation is by God's grace (and election), not by human efforts or merits.

64 What are election and predestination?

"Election" and "predestination" are often used as synonymous terms. They refer to salvation being established for humans by the power and grace of God rather than by human efforts in any form. It is God who determines or elects who will be saved and who will not be saved in a decree of predestination.

The view that election is entirely the work of God and not of humans was the common viewpoint of Luther, Zwingli, and Calvin. Sin ruptured the relationship between humans and God with sinful humans unable to draw or will themselves out of their sinful condition. So salvation is solely by God's grace, received by humans through the Holy Spirit's gift of faith. Among Reformation theologians and within the Lutheran and Reformed traditions, variations of views emerged as specific questions were answered in different ways.

One question related to the role of the electing God in relation to the condemnation or damnation of some. Zwingli spoke of God's "double decree"—a predestinating decree of salvation for some and damnation for others. Luther affirmed God's predestination to salvation—since humans have no "free will" to be able to accept the gospel by themselves. But Luther did not dwell on predestination and believed humans merited damnation because of their own rejection of the gospel.

For Calvin, there is God's election to salvation, and there is reprobation, or God's condemnation. Condemnation is due to God's just judgment on sinful people. Election is to be a comforting expression of God's grace, assuring those who believe in Christ that their salvation rests on the gracious and sustaining power of God rather than by the fragility of their own faith or actions.

The Lutheran Formula of Concord (1577) considers only an election to salvation, which is known through the Word of God, Jesus Christ. It rejects further speculation and urges believers to have hope for all. The Thirty-nine Articles of the Church of England (1563) spoke of the "unspeakable comfort" of election and did not mention a double predestination of salvation and condemnation.

65 What is justification?

Martin Luther made justification by faith a central issue of the Protestant Reformation.

Justification is a way of understanding salvation. It is especially presented throughout the letters of Paul in the New Testament, particularly in the books of Romans and Galatians, on which Luther lectured at the University of Wittenberg.

"Justification by faith alone" was Luther's slogan, drawn especially from Romans 1:17: "The righteousness of God is revealed through faith for faith; as it is written, 'The one who is righteous will live by faith.'" Justification is an image drawn from the law courts. Theologically it refers to the act of God in forgiving the sin of humanity on the basis of the righteousness of Jesus Christ—who was the sinless Son of God. Christ's death on the cross is accepted by God as the payment for the sins that humans have committed. Christ died for our sins. God accepts the righteousness of Christ as payment for human sin; and "accounts us righteous" on the basis of the "righteousness of Jesus Christ." This is God's action of free grace—giving sinful humans that which they do not deserve. Paul continued: ". . . but the free gift of God is eternal life in Christ Jesus our Lord" (Rom. 6:23). We receive this gift of grace—Jesus Christ's righteousness on our behalf—by faith. Then, "since we are justified by faith, we have peace with God through our Lord Jesus Christ" (Rom. 5:1).

The Protestant Reformers agreed that humans are justified by faith alone and not by works of the law through which humans would try to "earn" salvation by doing good works. This was the view of salvation associated with Roman Catholic teachings. The Reformers cited Paul: "For we hold that a person is justified by faith apart from works prescribed by the law" (Rom. 3:28). This formed the basis of two Reformation slogans: *grace alone* and *faith alone*.

66 What is faith?

Faith is key to the understanding of salvation and justification as understood by the Reformers.

Christian faith calls for faith in God whose grace and love is revealed in Jesus Christ. Faith indicates that which is believed— God is gracious and loving—as well as trust in a person—Jesus Christ. To have "faith" in Jesus Christ is to believe in Jesus and to trust Jesus.

Theologically, in Reformation theology, "faith" meant what is believed—specifically about Jesus Christ, who he is and what he is done—as well as one's trust and commitment in receiving the benefits of what Jesus Christ has done for us: in justification and salvation. In Anabaptist theology, a further emphasis is on faith as dying to sin and being raised to new life in Christ so that one can live a life of Christian discipleship. Thus, faith is centered on Jesus Christ; it is the gift of God, by God's grace (Eph. 2:8–9); it involves the whole person: intellect—what we believe; affections—whom we trust; and ethical action—living as disciples of Jesus Christ. Or, we could say: Head, Heart, and Hands. All this is known through the Scriptures.

Faith as a gift of God's Holy Spirit means faith is not self-generated. It is received and not earned. Faith is not something human reason can achieve by its own powers. Faith is the gift of God in which we receive the benefits of Jesus Christ. His death brings forgiveness of sins, liberation from the power of sin, and reconciliation and peace with God (2 Cor. 5:19; Rom. 5:1). In his resurrection, Christ was "raised for our justification" (Rom. 4:25).

In the Roman Catholic tradition, faith has been associated with baptism, which is called the sacrament of faith. Faith's focus in the late medieval period was on giving intellectual assent to what the church teaches and led to salvation only as it was formed by love in a person's life in a process of salvation.

These differing conceptions of the nature of faith marked Roman Catholic and Protestant teachings.

67 What good are "good works"?

In Reformation theology, salvation comes by God's grace through faith in Jesus Christ. Salvation is by "faith alone."

But for Protestants, this "faith alone" is not a "faith which is alone." That is, salvation in Jesus Christ always leads to the person who has faith doing "good works." Good works come as a response of faith, in gratitude to what God has done for us in Jesus Christ.

Theologically, good works are part of the process of sanctification (from Latin *sanctus*, "holy"), which is the Christian's growth in the Christian life. Justification leads to sanctification. Good works are ways one's salvation is expressed. Good works do not bring justification or salvation, they are fruits of faith, not the cause of faith. Luther said that good works do not make a person "good"—in the sense of being justified or saved. But a "good (justified) person" will do good works. Christians are "created in Christ Jesus for good works, which God prepared beforehand to be our way of life" (Eph. 2:10).

In this, the Protestant Reformers disagreed with the Roman Catholic view that when persons are baptized, God's grace leads them into doing good works. In this, they gain "merit" and thus salvation. "Merit" in classical Roman Catholicism meant that by God's grace God's reward is given as the human will works together with God to carry out actions that deserve or are worthy of God's favor.

The position of the Protestants was that intrinsically no human works can claim to be worthy of God's favor. God's reward for faithful actions may be given after death as an action of God's good pleasure (Calvin). But the good works done by Christians here and now do not have the power to bring salvation. They are *expressions* of salvation.

68 What is the church?

Questions about the nature of the church (and its sacraments) were divisive issues during the sixteenth-century Reformation.

The Protestant Reformers saw the church of Jesus Christ as a community of believers in Christ who are called together by the work of God's Holy Spirit. The church is constituted by God's eternal election of the saints, a particular emphasis of the Reformed tradition.

The church as the body of Christ is marked by the preaching of the Word of God and the right administration of the sacraments. A further mark of the church from the Scottish Reformation was that the church also administers church discipline. The Reformed discuss the church as the "invisible" church, that is, the saints whose faith is known only by God (the elect); and the "visible" church, which is the gathered Christian community that meets together and includes some members who may not have genuine faith in Jesus Christ. The Lutheran and Anglican traditions describe the church as where the gospel is preached purely and the pure Word of God is proclaimed. Luther maintained the church is created by God's Word, which brings faith in Jesus Christ.

The Reformers did not agree with the Roman Catholic view that the Roman church is the one, true church and is the dispenser of salvation. Here, participation in the Roman church is thus necessary for the salvation of any person. For outside the church there is no salvation. Participation in the church entitles one to receive the church's sacraments, which are the means by which the process of salvation takes place.

Anabaptist concerns were not with the "visible" and "invisible" church as much as with the visible church embodying true discipleship among its members. Like other Protestants, the

Anabaptists saw the church as founded on Christ and established through Scripture. But the first mark of true church was found in the new life of its members who lived as disciples of Christ.

69 What is preaching?

Preaching was central to the Reformation. The Protestant Reformers did not invent preaching. Prior to the Reformation, preaching orders existed in the Roman Catholic Church—Dominicans and Franciscans. John Wycliffe was a preacher and continued the preaching tradition.

The Reformation brought a new emphasis on biblical preaching. Major Reformers (except Melanchthon) were preachers and preached multiple times per week. Sermons from the Reformers fill many volumes of their works. Since the preaching of the Word is considered a mark of the church by the Reformers, preaching is the most important duty of a pastor.

The Reformers have differing emphases on the nature of preaching. But they agree that the preaching of the Word of God is the Word of God (Bullinger). Through the human preacher, God's Word is conveyed as the gospel (Luther)—to the congregation. Through the Holy Spirit, God uses the human words of the preacher to proclaim the Word of God—Jesus Christ and what he has done for our salvation. Preaching must be biblical (and theological) in nature since it is through the Bible as the revelation of God that we know of God's love in Jesus Christ. So preaching is "Word of God," as Scripture is "Word of God" and, primarily, Jesus Christ is "Word of God" (John 1:1).

God's Word in preaching is a *revealing* Word. Preaching's human words reveal God's divine Word, God's self-disclosure in Jesus Christ. God's Word in preaching is a *saving* Word, witnessing to the means of salvation. Through preaching, we become united with Christ by faith through the work of the Holy Spirit. God's Word in preaching is a *commanding* Word. Through preaching, Jesus Christ carries out divine authority in the church and over the world, as well as in the lives of believers. For the

Reformers, as for Paul: "Faith comes from what is heard, and what is heard comes through the word of Christ" (Rom. 10:17).

70 What is the priesthood of all believers?

One of the seven sacraments of the Roman Catholic Church is holy orders. In this, a man becomes a priest and carries out the sacraments of the church, which are considered essential for salvation. Priests lead worship, are celibate males, and function as mediators or intermediaries between God and humans. The priesthood and laity are completely separate from each other.

By 1520, Luther challenged this structure when he contended that all Christians were "priests" since they are believers in Jesus Christ. By baptism and their faith in the gospel of Christ, all Christians were spiritual priests (see 1 Cor. 12:12–13; 1 Pet. 2:9; Rev. 5:9–10). Clergy and laity had equal standing before God. This spiritual priesthood meant all Christians ministered to others. They can come directly to God through Jesus Christ without needing another person (clergy) as a mediator.

Further, the priesthood of all believers also meant the right to interpret Scripture. All Christians have the right and responsibility to judge what is true and untrue in Christian faith. Christians can judge, not being "subject" to others' views (1 Cor. 2:15) since all are spiritually united with Christ.

Yet the right to interpret Scripture for the church was entrusted to the Christian community as a whole. A strictly "private" interpretation of Scripture was not to be taken as the norm. For Luther, the church was to recognize the callings of some to proclaim the Word of God, teach, and administer sacraments. Those in the office of pastors are to interpret Scripture on behalf of the church. So while Luther rejected the Roman Church's hierarchy as the source for proper biblical interpretation, he also wanted to avoid a complete privatization of biblical interpretation by individual believers.

At the Council of Trent, the Roman Catholic Church rejected

the "priesthood of all believers" in favor of the church's traditional priestly structure.

71 What is ministry?

The Protestant Reformers with their emphasis on justification by God's grace through faith went on to affirm with the apostle Paul that faith is active through love (Gal. 5:6, 13). All Christians who are justified by faith participate in the priesthood of all believers in which they express faith to others by actions of love. This is service (Gk. *diakonia*) to others. It is what the Reformers understood as the nature of Christian ministry.

In this, the Reformers saw Jesus Christ as the model for ministry. His work of salvation meant giving his life for others; and serving others, as when Jesus said, "For the Son of Man came not to be served but to serve, and to give his life a ransom for many" (Mark 10:45). Jesus' ministry was of love and service to others: "I am among you as one who serves" (serve, service; Lat. *ministrat*; Luke 22:27).

This *ministry* of service is what all Christians are called to practice as an expression of their justification or salvation in Jesus Christ. Those who are called to ministries of Word and Sacrament in the church, particularly pastors, are to carry out their ministries not by seeking to be superior to others or gaining "celebrity status," as we would say, but by serving others. Again, Jesus said, "whoever wishes to be great among you must be your servant" (Matt. 20:26). Distinctions of position and rank disappear in the church by the equal standing of "clergy" and "laity." Their common unity is that they serve others as expressions of their love and faith in Jesus Christ.

This theological conviction that ministry was service fueled Reformation churches to enact ministries to the poor and those in need in addition to serving the needs through ministries of pastoral care. In the case of the church offices developed by Calvin, the office of deacon (from the Greek *diakonia*, "service") had especially vigorous roles in meeting human needs and organizing for the social welfare of the community.

72 What is Christian vocation?

The term "vocation," from the Latin *vocare*, "to call," was used in the medieval Roman Catholic Church to refer to those who participated in the monastic life or in the priesthood of the church. It is to those persons one could point to and say: Here are the truly "called" Christians.

Luther, however, believed that the New Testament taught that all Christians are "called." They are first called to be disciples of Jesus Christ, to be part of the "priesthood of all believers," through baptism and faith. This is a general call to all Christians. More specifically, Christians are called to a way of serving God in the particular station or role in life where one finds oneself. Appealing to 1 Corinthians 7:20, "Let each of you remain in the condition in which you were called," Luther saw these roles as static. One served God in Christ, perhaps as a farmer, merchant, etc. All such vocations were equal in dignity, even as they had differing social locations and status.

Calvin's view was more flexible. He too believed that the primary "call" or "calling" in the New Testament is to follow Christ. But to help us live out our Christian discipleship, God calls us to various forms of service—work or specific tasks. This form of vocation functions as a "sentry post" to help us express our faith and carry out the ministries God desires. These ministries and callings can change throughout the course of one's life, depending on the work of the Holy Spirit in leading one to new work or service. Our callings take shape in the midst of the world and the Christian's common life. They do not call one away from the world—as in the monastic model. Rather they are ways Christians can live out Paul's injunction: "Whatever you do, do everything for the glory of God" (1 Cor. 10:31).

The term "call" also came to be used for ratification of a particular form or place of ministry by ecclesiastical authorities, as when one is "called" to be pastor of a local church congregation.

73 What will be the end of all things?

"Eschatology" is the theological term referring to the "last things" (Gk. *eschatos*) or the end of the world. It has various dimensions relating to biblical and theological topics, including the second coming of Christ, the Last Judgment, the eternal reign of Christ, and the kingdom of God, as well other themes.

In the medieval period, figures such as Joachim of Fiore (c. 1135–1202) and Girolamo Savonarola (1452–1498) stirred eschatological excitement with their prophetical and mystical teachings. Many expected that the second coming of Christ would occur and that Christ would set up his millennial kingdom to rule over the earth (see Rev. 20:2–7). Apocalypticism was the view that eschatology was ready to happen at any moment.

During the early Reformation period, there was widespread belief that the "last days" were occurring and that the end of the world would happen soon. Anabaptist theologians often made forecasts. Hans Hut predicted the world would end in 1528 and Melchior Hoffman in 1534. The attempt to establish a holy kingdom at Münster (1534–1535), which would become the new Jerusalem (Rev. 3:12; 21:2, 10), was a sign of the restoration of the gospel and of the imminent return of Christ. After the devastating end of the Münster experience, Anabaptists no longer emphasized eschatological elements in the same way.

Luther and other Reformers saw signs of the end of the world in events of their times. The identification of the pope as antichrist— the "man of sin" (1 John 2:18, 22; 4:3; 2 John 1:7; cf. 2 Thess. 2:3)—was a common sign that the end was near. For Luther, threats by the Turks (1529) also brought heightened expectations of the world's end. Yet, at times, Luther was more optimistic that the world would proceed on its course as God continued to work.

Calvin emphasized God's sovereignty and proclaimed that God's purposes were being worked out in history. History was moving toward God's ultimate reign. The church awaits God's final reign, a reign that has begun as the ascended Christ in his resurrection embodies glorified humanity. Christians should meditate on the future life, enabling them to endure present-day sufferings as they anticipate sharing in Christ's glory.

74 What about life after death?

Whether there is life after death is a question that arises for many people. Christians find support for life after death in the Scriptures. But there have been disagreements about different aspects of the concept.

In the Reformation period, all groups generally agreed that there is life after death, either in heaven—for Christian believers—or in hell—for those who have rejected the gospel.

In the Roman Catholic tradition, purgatory is an initial destination after death. It is a place where people who were not terrifically evil but who owed debts to God at their death spend time being painfully purified before they go to heaven. The devout were to pray for souls in purgatory, and indulgences could be purchased on their behalf. The indulgence controversy launched Luther's reformatory activities. But the idea of purgatory has been rejected among Protestant churches.

In Protestantism, heaven is the place of ultimate blessedness, being the dwelling place of God, the Holy Trinity. It is the eternal destination of the elect of God, those of the invisible church (Reformed tradition), those who have received salvation through Jesus Christ. It is the direct destination of the saved after their death and the Last Judgment. The concept of "soul sleep" or a period between death and entrance to heaven was rejected by most Protestants. The uniting of "soul" and "body" has been a historic feature of Protestant thought, to occur at the final resurrection.

Hell is the destination of the unsaved, after the Last Judgment. The Reformers saw it as an expression of God's justice and the proper judgment on human sin that violates God's law and cuts sinful humanity off from a relationship of trust, love, and obedience to God—the results of original sin. Hell is the place of eternal punishment. Some have taken biblical images such as fire (Matt. 5:22; 18:9) literally, with hell being the place "where their worm never dies, and the fire is never quenched" (Mark 9:48).

6

Dividing Issues among Protestants

75 **What are differences in worship among Protestants?**

Christian worship is offered to the triune God. It is the service of God's glory. Protestant worship emphasizes the offering of the self to God in faith and in gratitude for God's gracious love in Jesus Christ. Worship is the work of the Holy Spirit in gathering the community of believers together and in working within the assembled congregation and in human hearts. Protestant worship is marked by the proclamation of the Word of God, based on the written Word (Scripture), and is focused on the living Word, Jesus Christ.

Lutheran traditions have permitted worship elements commanded in Scripture and those not explicitly forbidden. Reformed traditions have emphasized conforming worship to what is given in Scripture as worship elements. A middle ground is struck in the Church of England's Thirty-nine Articles, which provide that the church has power to use rites and ceremonies that are not contrary to Scripture (art. 20) while also indicating that traditions and ceremonies may change according to diversities in countries, times, and manners (art. 34). Anabaptist worship has focused on the church as the visible community of Christ whose members carried the Holy Spirit into the world in witness. Liturgical forms emerged from congregational practice.

Reading Scripture, preaching, prayers, and singing have been ongoing component parts of Protestant worship. Each has a distinctive role to play in the worship service. Yet specific forms of these rubrics have varied. For example, Protestants have disagreed on whether prayers should be scripted or spontaneous? English Puritans thought that the written prayers of the *Book of Common Prayer* lacked a deep spiritual quality and were "read" rather than rightly "prayed." Through the years, many Protestants have maintained room for both approaches to prayers.

Protestant worship has adapted in various ways through the centuries depending on its contexts and many other features. What is primary throughout is that worship is given as praise to God. Worship is not focused on human "performance" or glorification.

76 Can salvation be lost?

Theologians in the Reformed tradition and Reformed churches have understood Scripture to teach that those who are saved by God's grace in Jesus Christ cannot lose their salvation. This is called "perseverance" or the "perseverance of the saints."

The medieval Roman Catholic Church taught that though persons continued to participate in the sacraments of the church, which is necessary for salvation, it was possible for salvation to be lost and that believers could fall from grace.

During the Reformation period, this was considered at the Synod of Dort (1618–1619). The Arminian view was that it was possible for believers to backslide or lose their salvation after they had made an initial commitment of faith in Jesus Christ.

John Calvin had emphasized the perseverance of the elect, or Christian believers, rests in the power of God. This was the position of the Reformed at Dort. This meant that those of the elect who may drift away from the faith at some points will be restored to faith by God's grace. Those who make an initial commitment to Christ but turn away from the faith completely and do not return are not of the elect.

The elect do sin, and faith is no guarantee of a trouble-free life. But faith continues through difficulties. The assurance of Jesus is primary: "I give them eternal life, and they will never perish. No one will snatch them out of my hand" (John 10:28).

The Reformed have emphasized salvation is by God's power and initiative—in election and in coming to faith in Christ by the work of the Holy Spirit. What God has begun in justification, God will continue through sanctification unto glorification. As Paul wrote, "the one who began a good work among you will bring it to completion by the day of Jesus Christ" (Phil. 1:6).

77 What did Reformers understand as a sacrament?

The Latin term *sacramentum* means "oath" or "vow." Historically, the Roman Catholic Church has believed that sacraments are rites ordained by Christ or his apostles to convey divine grace to believers. From the twelfth century, the Roman Catholic Church recognized seven sacraments: baptism, confirmation, penance, Eucharist (Lord's Supper), marriage, holy orders (ordination to the priesthood), and extreme unction (anointing of the sick).

Luther and other Reformers reduced the number to two, baptism and the Lord's Supper, since these were instituted by Christ and were for all persons. Controversies arose over baptism—whether it should be administered to infants or to adult believers who confess their faith. Controversies over the Lord's Supper centered on the nature of Christ's presence in the Supper: whether it was a "true" (Calvin) and "real" presence (Lutheran and Roman Catholic) or "spiritual" and "memorial" (Zwingli). Reformation Christians considered a correct view of the sacraments as an essential Christian belief.

Reformation theology saw sacraments as outward signs of an inward or invisible grace (Augustine). Sacraments do not provide automatic efficacy or benefits. They must be received in faith. So they are thus beneficial only to believers in Christ.

Luther and the Anglican tradition taught that sacraments involved (1) a sign or symbol as well as (2) actual grace, conferred by God. In the Reformed tradition, Calvin and others saw that in a sacrament, there was (1) the sign or symbol; (2) the "thing symbolized," which exists in a union with the sign or symbol; and (3) the

Holy Spirit who works in conjunction with the words of institution for the sacrament to seal God's grace within us. Sacraments are signs and seals. All is received in faith.

Zwingli's view of sacraments was that they were memorial signs that functioned as public testimonies to one's faith. They did not convey grace but helped one remember grace while participants witness to the world that they are people of faith. In Anabaptism, sacraments were not conveyors of grace but were ordinances that were testimonies to faith. The Roman Catholic Council of Trent directly rejected all Protestant viewpoints.

78 What were Reformers' views of baptism?

Protestants, except for Anabaptists, concur that baptism is a sacrament, agreeing with the Roman Catholic tradition that it is properly administered to infants, as well as adults who confess their faith in Jesus Christ as Lord and Savior. Baptism incorporates one into the body of Christ, the church community.

Protestant agreements on the nature of baptism did not extend to consensus on the correct form for baptism. Luther believed a "seed of faith" was given to infants in baptism. Baptism was not necessary for salvation for Luther, and he rejected the Roman Catholic view of "limbo" (Lat. *limbus infantum*, "borderland of infants"), a place for the souls of unbaptized children.

Zwingli, in accord with his view of sacraments, regarded baptism as a symbolic initiation into the Christian community. Calvin, too, saw baptism as entrance into the Christian community. But he believed baptism was a visible sign of the inward working of God's grace. The faith of those who stood with the child—parents, the gathered community—represented the faith response that enabled the sacrament to convey God's grace. Baptism was a sacrament of the church, the gathered community where the Holy Spirit was at work.

Infant baptism was defended by Calvin and Bullinger. They saw it as a sign of God's covenant, a counterpart to circumcision, which was the entrance into the community of Israel in the Old Testament. Baptism is a "spiritual circumcision" (Col. 2:11). In baptism, God's promises are sealed within us, confirming our sins are forgiven.

Anabaptists insisted that a public profession of faith in Christ must precede baptism. Thus baptism could be administered only to adults and not to infants who cannot make this confession. Adult, or "Believer's Baptism," became a defining mark of the Radical Reformation. Sixteenth-century governmental authorities saw this rejection of infant baptism as a sign of potential disruptions in society.

In response to Protestant views of baptism, the Council of Trent reaffirmed the Roman church's belief in seven sacraments as well as the view that baptism forgave original sin and was necessary for salvation.

79 Why was the Lord's Supper a divisive issue?

Different views of the nature of a sacrament were expressed most clearly in the divergences among the Reformers on the Lord's Supper. Most particularly, the issue of the nature of the presence of Christ in the Supper proved to be a decisive stumbling block to potential Protestant unity, as the Colloquy of Marburg (1529) demonstrated.

This is ironic—and tragic. The Lord's Supper was instituted by Jesus to bind his community of faith together. Jesus had prayed "that they may all be one" (John 17:21). Yet that unity in Christ, represented in the common meal of the Supper as Jesus prepared to give himself for the "sin of the world" (John 1:29), became the most divisive issue of the Protestant Reformation.

The differing views of the major Reformers related to their understanding of Christology, particularly the nature of who Jesus Christ is after his resurrection and ascension to heaven. How Christ can be "present"—or not—in the Lord's Supper is an expression of convictions about the person of Jesus Christ.

What united Protestants theologically was a rejection of the Roman Catholic view of transubstantiation. The words of Jesus, "This is my body . . . this is my blood" (Mark 14:22, 24), were interpreted literally in Roman Catholic theology. When the priest says these words, the words of institution, in the Mass, the inner reality of the elements of the bread and wine are transformed. Their "substance" was changed. There is no outward change to their appearance ("accidents"); but they "become" the body and blood of Christ. This view is called transubstantiation. The priest presented the sacrifice of Jesus Christ anew with each celebration of the Mass.

The Reformers had their own ways of understanding what happens in the Lord's Supper. But they agreed that the metaphysical change of the elements, represented in the doctrine of transubstantiation, was not true to the New Testament. Because the Reformers believed it was crucial to understand the nature of the Lord's Supper as a key element of Christian faith, they strongly maintained the rightness of their particular beliefs.

80   What did Lutherans believe about the Lord's Supper?

Luther wrote against the Roman Catholic view of the Lord's Supper (Eucharist). One of his major criticisms was against what he believed was a "mechanical" view of the Supper in Roman Catholic theology. There the sacrament was said to work *ex opere operato*. That is, "from the work done." The sacrament gains its power from being done in the proper manner by the priest. The sacrament conveys grace to everyone who is not in the state of mortal sin.

Luther's view was that the sacrament is effective only when it is received by faith in those who receive the elements, the bread and the wine (Lat. *ex opere operantis*; "out of [by] the work of the worker"). The Supper is a direct address from God that must be received in faith for its power to be received.

Luther rejected the Roman view that the substance of the

elements is changed in the Supper (transubstantiation). But Luther argued for the bodily presence of Christ in the Supper. Christ is present in the untransformed elements. The church proclaims that in Jesus Christ, "the Word became flesh" (John 1:14). God became a human being. So, in the Supper, said Luther, the church proclaims that God dwells "in" and "under" the bread and wine. What is true of Christ is true of the Supper. Christ's presence is real and surrounds the elements. "This is my body," Jesus said (Mark 14:22). The risen, ascended Christ is ubiquitous; that is, Christ is present in his divine and human nature everywhere—at all times. This means at all celebrations of the Lord's Supper.

Christ's real and personal presence in the Supper was the crucial point of difference between Luther and Zwingli, as the Marburg Colloquy (1529) showed. For Luther, the Supper contained Jesus' promise of the forgiveness of sins. In some ways, the Supper was an extension of the incarnation—God becoming a human in Jesus Christ. God was present in Christ in the Supper, as Christ is present, "in, with, and under" the elements. Though Luther did not use the term as later Lutherans did, this view is sometimes called "consubstantiation." Christ's presence surrounds the sacrament.

81 What did the Zwinglians believe about the Lord's Supper?

Zwingli and Luther came to an impasse on the Lord's Supper at the Marburg Colloquy (1529) over the issue of Christ's presence in the Supper.

For Zwingli, the Supper is a testimony to faith and trust in God. It is not, primarily, about Christ's presence in the bread and wine. The term "Eucharist" means "thanksgiving." This is what the Supper was about for Zwingli. It is a thanksgiving and a rejoicing by the Christian community that is remembering and declaring the death of Christ.

Zwingli saw a sharp contrast between "spirit" and "flesh." He said that John 6 was the place to look to find a true meaning for the Eucharist. Jesus said, "It is the spirit that gives life; the flesh is useless. The words that I have spoken to you are spirit and life" (John 6:63; cf. "What is born of the flesh is flesh, and what is born of the Spirit is spirit," John 3:6). This meant, said Zwingli, that the earthly, visible, material world ("flesh") cannot be the bearer of the salvation that comes by God's Spirit. The material world points beyond itself—like the spoken words and elements in the Supper— to the salvation reality that is greater than the "flesh." So when Jesus spoke of eating his flesh and drinking his blood (1 Cor. 11:23–26), he must have been speaking symbolically or metaphorically, not literally. The words are symbols for believing in Christ, or having faith. Eating is believing. "This is my body" means "this signifies my body." Christ had ascended to heaven and could not be bodily present in the celebrations of the Supper on earth.

Christ's spiritual presence at the Supper is in the hearts of those who believe in him for salvation. As believers contemplate their faith, hope, and love—found in Christ—they rejoice in thanksgiving (eucharist). The elements are only "signs" and are not themselves what the elements signify. A sacrament does not communicate God's grace, it commemorates it. Zwingli's views are sometimes called "memorialism" since the Supper is a memorial, or a bringing to memory, the salvation believers have in Jesus Christ.

82 What did followers of Calvin believe about the Lord's Supper?

Calvin's emphasis on the Lord's Supper was on the "for you," when Jesus said, "This is my body that is for you" (1 Cor. 11:24). He stressed the spiritual union of believers with Christ, by the power of the Holy Spirit, rather than focusing on the relation of Christ to the elements of the Lord's Supper.

Calvin believed, against Zwingli, that the signs in a sacrament communicate the reality they symbolize. Calvin thought Luther, though rejecting transubstantiation, still emphasized too heavily the outward signs by speaking of Christ's presence surrounding them. In this regard, Calvin's views are often seen as a middle ground or median between the other two Reformers.

Like Zwingli, Calvin believed that the ascended Christ was

present "at the right hand of God" in heaven. So Christ is not "locally present" at all the celebrations of the Lord's Supper in all churches. Instead, Calvin's emphasis was that Christ is spiritually present in the Supper for believers, wherever it is celebrated. This happens by the work of the Holy Spirit who feeds believers with the benefits Christ has promised and brought in salvation (this view is sometimes called "virtualism"—the benefits or "virtues" of Christ's death are communicated). The Supper is a mystery since we cannot see or comprehend or express *how* the benefits of Christ are communicated to believers, apart from the witness of the promises of Scripture. We can only wonder, in praise. In the church community, Christ is truly present, proclaiming the love and salvation he brings, as believers are united with Christ by faith in the Supper and nourished by Christ's sacrifice unto eternal life: "This is my body that is *for you*" (1 Cor. 11:24; italics added).

So the Supper, and the sacraments, sustain, nourish, confirm, and increase faith in believers. The Spirit lifts our hearts on high into the presence of the ascended Christ in heaven, who fills "all things" (Eph. 4:10). As the Word of God is proclaimed, so the Spirit of God is at work. God uses the common elements of bread and wine to be the means by which, through faith, we receive the benefits of Christ's work of salvation—"for us." The "spiritual banquet" of the Supper is effective only for those who have faith, which is a gift of the Holy Spirit (to God's elect). Faith falters in believers. The Supper is a medicine for those who are sick, hope for the sinners, and spiritual nourishment for the Christian life. Jesus Christ is the host of the Supper, giving himself. In the Supper, by faith, believers receive the sign and the seal of Christ's work, by the power of the Holy Spirit.

83 What did Anabaptists believe about the Lord's Supper?

Anabaptists adopted a Zwinglian view of sacraments and thus rejected the bodily presence of Christ in the Lord's Supper. They believed the ascended, glorified Christ is at "the right hand of God," where he will be until he returns to judge the earth.

Anabaptists enacted the Last Supper of Jesus with his disciples in anticipation of the coming messianic banquet, promised by Jesus (Luke 13:29). The Supper served as a sign and memorial, as Zwingli emphasized. It looked back to Christ's saving death on the cross as being a sign of the future kingdom of Christ, which is the kingdom of his grace. The Supper was a witness or testimony to Christ's love for us, shown on the cross, and shown in the lives of Christ's disciples daily, as God's acts of grace. This love is actively at work in believers who participate in the Supper, renewing their faith as they resolve to be more faithful in their discipleship. What is most important is what occurs within the experience of believers. Joy and peace flood the heart as praise and thanksgiving are offered to God. This emphasis is a heightening of what takes place in the experience of those who participate in the Supper rather than on the presence of Christ in a theologically described way, as with Luther.

Ethical dimensions of the Lord's Supper were part of the Anabaptist perspectives. The Supper was a bond of Christian unity, love, and peace. Participants had to lay aside quarrels and contentions, to forgive one another, and to be active in reproving and exhorting fellow Christians. Their ultimate commitment in self-denial was to be ready to die for their faith. These emerged from the communion (Gk. *koinōnia*; fellowship, sharing) of the body and blood of Christ, represented in the Supper.

Some Anabaptist groups also practiced the ordinance of footwashing, according to Jesus' command (John 13:14). This represented cleansing by Christ and established the true humility to which the Supper calls believers.

84 What did the Church of England believe about the Lord's Supper?

Those in the Church of England are instructed by the Thirty-nine Articles of faith. These reflect the influence of Thomas Cranmer and are understood in conjunction with the *Book of Common Prayer,* which guides liturgical usage.

Cranmer's views on the Lord's Supper have been the subject of debate with portions of his writings being used to support a "Zwinglian" understanding and others a perspective more in line with Luther. Cranmer spoke of the Supper as being a memorial of Christ's sacrifice with Christ's natural body, which is in heaven not in the bread. Yet also, Christ is really present—a true presence. The purpose of the Supper is for the ascended Christ to feed and nurture his people.

The Thirty-nine Articles reject transubstantiation as repugnant to Scripture. They affirm the body of Christ is given, taken, and eaten in the Supper, after a heavenly and spiritual manner (not in a locally present manner, as with Luther). The means by which the body of Christ is received this way, and eaten in the Supper, is faith.

These Articles of Religion do not seek to explain how Christ is present in the Supper. The mode of Christ's presence is a mystery, which cannot be fully defined. The revised *Book of Common Prayer* (1559), promulgated under Queen Elizabeth, combined the two earlier books (1549; 1552) for the words of the priest in serving the bread in Communion: "The body of our Lord Jesus Christ, which was given for thee, preserve thy body and soul until everlasting life: and take and eat this in remembrance that Christ died for thee, feed on him in thine heart by faith, with thanksgiving." Here, an identification of the bread with Christ's body is followed by urging the believer to take the bread to remember Christ's work.

By 1597, Richard Hooker indicated that there was a general agreement in the Church of England of a real participation of Christ and of Christian life in his body and blood, which the sacrament of the Lord's Supper brings. Church of England theology struck a "middle way" (*via media*) in the Reformation debates.

85 What are the major forms of church government?

Reformation churches established several different forms of church polity, or the structure of church government.

Episcopal. The Roman Catholic Church practices the episcopal form of church government, the term coming from the Greek word *episkopos*, which means "overseer," and in Latin *episcopus*, "bishop." Bishops play a central role in governing the church. In the Roman system, the bishop of Rome (pope) stands at the head of the college of bishops. Eastern Orthodox churches also have an episcopal polity. In Reformation churches, the Church of England and Anglican churches practice an episcopal polity and have a threefold ministry of deacons, priests, and bishops. This hierarchical model descends from the "head" to the "members."

Presbyterian. Many Reformed churches have practiced a presbyterian polity. The term "presbyterian" comes from the Greek word, *presbyteros*, meaning "elder." Reformed churches and those called Presbyterian churches practice a polity by which the church is governed by elders. In local congregations, the session (sometimes "consistory") is composed of laity, called "elders." Some denominations refer to "teaching elders" (pastors) and "ruling elders" (laity). In French Reformed churches of the 1550s, local churches were governed by the session; a regional assembly, the presbytery (sometimes "classis"), was pastors and elders from the region's local church sessions. Groups of representatives from a presbytery formed a synod; and the General Assembly was representatives from the national church.

Congregational. Anabaptist churches as they became established practiced a congregational form of polity where the local congregation is the principal expression of the church. Local churches with their pastors may have local leaders. But this pattern gives decisions on church doctrine and practice to the local congregation.

Some Reformed churches practice a congregational form of polity. Various Lutheran churches have adopted different polities. Many have bishops, some have overseers called "superintendents" (the same oversight function as the Greek *episkopos*). Some Lutheran churches have a modified form of congregational polity.

The purpose of all church government is to enable churches to carry out their ministries in ways that give glory to God.

86 What did Reformers believe about church and state?

The Reformation brought a number of questions about the proper spheres and relationships between civil and ecclesiastical authority.

Luther's doctrine of the "two kingdoms" differentiated two realms: the kingdom of God and the kingdom of the world. God rules through both realms, through the gospel and commands of Jesus in the kingdom of God, and in the kingdom of the world through secular government. Governments punish those who do evil and exist to preserve societal peace. The kingdom of God proclaims the gospel and establishes God's rule in human hearts. A Christian is subject to secular authority, but obedience is not due to unjust governments. Christians may name injustices but not resist authority with force.

Zwingli, in Zurich, maintained that boundaries between civil society and the church community were fluid. He and his successor, Bullinger, held to a single sphere instead of "two kingdoms." For them, a Christian city is a Christian congregation. God's moral law is the divine will for all people and forms the basis for laws of society. Zwingli believed that elders of the New Testament were equivalents of Christian magistrates in his own time. So in a Christian city, the council of the city rightfully ruled the civil community as well as the church. Excommunication should reside with the council and be used only against open sinners.

Calvin in Geneva wanted to maintain separate bodies of the city's governing body (the council) and the church. Their duties did not usually overlap. Together, church and state are to establish a society where justice and works of compassion are enacted, the needs of the poor are met, and peace is maintained. Church discipline is carried out by church bodies.

Reformed adherents were sometimes branded as "revolutionary" (the Netherlands, France, England). Calvin's theology allowed for resistance by "lesser magistrates." This became extended by later followers and opened possibilities for more active resistance and for political revolution for some, with the English Civil War becoming an example.

Anabaptists focused on Jesus' Sermon on the Mount and believed that Christians should not participate in governmental roles. They saw a sharp dichotomy between the kingdom of this world and Christian discipleship. The Christian stance is to be pacifism.

The church/state issue continues to be an underlying issue in every society.

Legacy

7

Reformation Heritage

87 **What did the Reformation contribute to social ethics?**

A basic foundation for Christian social ethics emerged from an emphasis of the Reformers on the "second Table" of the Law (commandments 6 through 10 of the Ten Commandments) and the command Jesus reinforced that his followers are to "love your neighbor as yourself" (Mark 12:31; cf. Lev. 19:18). This set a biblical basis for the focus of Christian ethics and actions. It established love as a primary motivation for what Christians should say and do and ways the teachings and ethic of Jesus are to be expressed in Christian relationships and actions. Protestant theologians were critical of Roman Catholic use of "natural law" as a part of the foundational basis for Christian ethics.

The Christian community acts in Christian love on the basis of God's grace in Jesus Christ. This love—along with justice, which is to accompany it—is a result of grace. Luther's basic formula that good works follow justification by faith meant good works are done on behalf of others, especially those in need. Calvin emphasized that the command to love our neighbors means loving all people. The answer to the lawyer's question to Jesus, "Who is my neighbor?" (Luke 10:29) is everyone! "Neighbor" is not limited to those near to us; it reaches out to embrace all persons. For everyone is created in the image of God (Gen. 1:26–27).

Social-ethical concerns in Reformation cities were founded in concerns for relief for the poor. For many Protestants, participation in governmental structures that sought the well-being of citizens was a means of expressing love for others in societal forms.

Some theologians in Reformation traditions probed ethical issues in "cases of conscience," which posed ethical questions and sought to answer them on the basis of a theological understanding of Scripture.

In the broad sense, social ethics—as well as all ethical thought and action—are to be expressions of the church's theology, or as Paul put it, "faith working through love" (Gal. 5:6; cf. Jas. 2:14, 22–23).

88 What is the Reformation's relation to social welfare?

Christian faith expressed in good works of love and service to others took place in the Reformation period in acts of individual care. They were also enacted in broader attempts to serve others by providing for the welfare of groups of people in cities.

Before the Reformation, aid for the poor was offered by institutions that provided alms (food or coin) as well as shelters. Cathedrals and parishes churches distributed alms and bread to those in need.

As Protestants gained political authority and "became Protestant," care for the poor and the social welfare of the community were carried out by the "secular" governments, usually city councils. This social welfare was seen as part of the government's work, as governments sought to articulate their policies. Governments could centralize poor relief and carry it out more effectively than a number of smaller entities. Among the kinds of care established were hospitals, soup kitchens, schools, orphanages, and shelters. In Roman Catholic cities, governments took on more of a supervisory instead of "hands-on" roles.

In Geneva, Calvin indicated that deacons were one of the four church offices (pastor, teacher, elder, and deacon). Deacons were responsible for caring for the poor and those suffering physically. Their two functions were to administer benevolence and to care personally for those in need. The *Bourse française* or "the French fund for poor foreigners" was for the hundreds of Protestant refugees who came to Geneva during Calvin's time. Calvin worked with city authorities to establish an organizational structure for charity. This became the fundamental institution in Geneva, along with the disciplinary body, the consistory, and the Venerable Company of Pastors.

In contrast to the Roman Catholic view that giving alms to the poor counted toward the remission of punishment for sin, which would otherwise need to be purged in purgatory, the Protestants emphasized that charity is expressed as a response of love to God and of one's neighbor.

89 What is the Reformation's relation to modern science?

The rise of modern science is generally seen as originating in seventeenth-century Europe. This followed the tumultuous period of the sixteenth-century Reformation when reform of the church could be seen to have ripple effects for the reform of other aspects of human life and thought, including science.

This has led to speculation about to what degree Protestantism had an impact on the emergence of modern science. To what degree might the doctrines and practices of Protestantism have encouraged the development of scientific inquiry across a range of the disciplines we today call "the sciences"? Proposed answers to these questions are complex and nuanced.

Among aspects explored by scholars in considering these questions are elements of Protestantism that include: (1) the Protestant work ethic, stressing the calling of Christians to do work for the glory of God, including enhancing understandings of the world in all its aspects; (2) the need for the empirical observation of nature as an expression of God's choices and thus "natural law" and the "laws of nature"; (3) Protestant views of humanity where the effects of sin mean humans cannot clearly see how nature is functioning and thus there is the need for experimentation and an experimental approach to nature; (4) the literal sense of Scripture that was emphasized by the Reformers and that later encouraged scientists such as Francis Bacon and others in the British Royal Society to pursue the quest to understand "the first man" and other origins as a scientific motivation; and (5) physico-theology, which represents attempts to relate "natural theology" to "revealed theology"—God as known and revealed in nature compared to God's revelation in Scripture and in Jesus Christ. Reformation emphases on God's revelation in Scripture can mean a freedom to examine and study nature and the natural world to discover the wisdom and power of God.

These early, formative influences have now taken different and evolving shapes in the developments of modern science to the present time. At points, those committed to forms of Protestantism, especially in fundamentalist forms, have seen science as in conflict with faith. For others, science and theology are seen as complementary efforts in developing a more holistic view of God and the world around us.

90 What is the Reformation's relation to capitalism?

Capitalism is an economic theory that urges that the free flow of goods in the marketplace, which is not impeded by or subject to governmental control, best serves economic well-being. As individuals or groups compete for markets, those who will be best rewarded are those who maximize their profits while minimizing their production costs.

The relation of Protestantism and capitalism was the subject of a classic work by the German intellectual, Max Weber (1864–1920). In *The Protestant Ethic and the Spirit of Capitalism* (1905), Weber argued that values stemming from Calvinistic Protestantism shaped the world that is driven by capitalism. To gain assurance of their election (salvation), Protestants developed a work ethic—an "ascetic Protestantism," according to Weber, in which work was done for the sake of work. When success resulted, a "capitalist spirit" developed, and one had proof one was carrying out God's purposes and thus had evidence of one's election. This drive helped transform the Western world, said Weber.

Historians and other critics have claimed that Weber's theory is oversimplified and does not account for other important factors, such as that Roman Catholics as well as Calvinists were able to thrive in post-medieval society. Also, Calvin himself was suspicious of making profits that led to the neglect of humans in need.

A Protestant theological perspective on Weber's theory is that God is sovereign, the Lord of all. So all economic systems and human motivations or desires stand under God's judgment. When one commits, uncritically, to any human theory or method so that it becomes all-encompassing, idolatry is the result. This denies the sovereignty of God since it drives one to a relentless pursuit of one's own will and plans without subjecting these to God's will.

91 Who are the descendants of Luther?

Followers of Martin Luther began to establish Lutheran churches. These led to a family of Lutheran bodies established throughout the world today.

The Lutheran World Federation (LWF), a communion of Lutheran churches, represents over seventy-two million Christians in ninety-eight countries throughout the world. Churches united in the federation subscribe to the federation's doctrinal standard derived from historical documents from Lutheran history that are considered to be right expositions of Holy Scripture, which is the source and norm of the church's life. In the United States, the Lutheran Church—Missouri Synod and some of its associated churches are not members of the LWF.

Lutheran churches maintain a fidelity to the teachings of Luther and the work of Luther's chief colleague, Philipp Melanchthon. Soon after Luther's death, from approximately 1580 to 1700, a period of confessionalism and orthodoxy marked Lutheran theology. Lutheran theologians such as Matthias Flacius (1520–1575), Martin Chemnitz (1522–1586), Johann Gerhard (1582–1637),

Johannes Andreas Quenstedt (1617–1688), and others provided detailed theological works. These theologians especially critiqued the Roman Catholic theology of the Council of Trent as well as presenting clearly Luther's thought as it was further developed. Rich devotional literature, as well as the tradition of hymns—which Luther loved—also continued to unfold in this period. This period of Lutheran Orthodoxy also featured the appearance of Lutheran catechisms.

The Leuenberg Concord (1973) marked a joint declaration with Reformed churches to say that historical disagreements about the Lord's Supper between the two communions are no longer considered sufficient reasons to prevent church fellowship among churches in Germany. The LWF also reached an agreement with the Roman Catholic Church that historical condemnations of each other's doctrine of justification are no longer endorsed. This was expressed in the *Joint Declaration on the Doctrine of Justification* and its "Annex" (1999). Lutherans have made significant contributions to the wider ecumenical movement in the twentieth and twenty-first centuries.

92 Who are the descendants of Zwingli and Calvin?

Churches in the Reformed theological tradition tracing their origins to Zwingli and Calvin in the Reformation period continue today throughout the world. The global organization, the World Communion of Reformed Churches (WCRC), was formed in 2010 as a successor to the World Alliance of Reformed Churches (WARC). It is a fellowship (Gk. *koinōnia*) of Congregational, Presbyterian, Reformed, United, Uniting, and Waldensian churches. Over 225 member churches from over one hundred countries, embracing some eighty million Christians, belong to the WCRC.

Calvin's successor in Geneva, Theodore Beza (1519–1605), and Zwingli's successor in Zurich, Heinrich Bullinger (1504–1575), continued to expand Reformed theology. Parallel to developments in Lutheran theology, a period of orthodoxy, or scholasticism, developed from the late sixteenth into the eighteenth centuries. This featured the works of a number of theologians, including Beza, Girolamo Zanchi (1516–1590), Amandus Polanus (1561–1610), Francis Turretin (1623–1687), and others. Their concerns were to develop more detailed theological responses to Roman Catholicism as well as to the scholastic Lutheran theologians of the period.

The Reformed tradition of churches is marked by a number of confessional documents that emerged from the various localities where Reformed churches were found. Among these were The Lausanne Articles (1536), The French Confession (1559), The Belgic Confession (1561), The Heidelberg Catechism (1563), The Second Helvetic Confession (1566), and the Westminster Standards (1647). The Reformed stance toward confessions of faith has been to maintain their roots in the church's tradition while also being open to being "further reformed" according to the Word of God and the guidance of the Holy Spirit. This is captured by an unofficial Reformed motto: "The church reformed and always being reformed, according to the Word of God." The Reformed impetus to confess Christian faith in a Reformed manner continues to the present with new confessional statements often appearing.

Reformed churches have been involved in ecumenical discussions with many other Christian bodies throughout the world, including Anglicans, Lutherans, Pentecostals, and Roman Catholics. The WCRC organizes its work around justice, leadership development, mission, and theology.

93 Who are descendants of the Anglicans?

The Church of England, established through the English Reformation, continues to exist today. Anglicanism is the term for churches in relation to the Church of England, existing in some thirty-eight national or regional churches in over 165 countries throughout the world. These constitute the Anglican Communion, encompassing about eighty-five million Christians. They are united in their being in communion with the Archbishop of Canterbury, the bishop of the founding see (center of authority of a bishop). In some places these churches are referred to as Episcopal churches.

Anglican churches have seen themselves as bridge churches between Roman Catholicism and Eastern Orthodoxy on one hand and Protestantism on the other. Anglicans have maintained essential doctrines of the Protestant Reformation, including justification by grace through faith. Yet, historically, the Church of England has seen itself as maintaining the catholicity of the church in that the early English Reformation was not trying to establish a "new" church but rather to reform the Christian church that went back to the apostles. In that regard, elements such as the ancient threefold ministry—deacons, priests, and bishops—was maintained along with an episcopal form of church government and traditional symbols used in worship, including vestments, use of the sign of the cross, and other elements. The church adheres to the Thirty-nine Articles but does not have a strong sense of confessional identity, by the use of multiple statements of faith, as with Lutheranism and the Reformed tradition. Historically, there has been a breadth of tolerance within the Anglican communion of churches.

The *Book of Common Prayer* continues as the worship resource that unites the Anglican communion. Anglican liturgy today is shaped by the *Book of Common Prayer* as well as elements of twentieth-century liturgical renewal movements.

The Anglican communion continues to be involved in ecumenical dialogues with other traditions.

94 Who are the descendants of the Anabaptists?

Anabaptists in the Reformation period wished to go beyond the reforms advocated by Luther, Zwingli, Bucer, and Calvin. Distinctively, they rejected the practice of infant baptism as practiced by the Roman Catholic and other Reformation church bodies. They maintained baptism should follow a confession of faith in Jesus Christ, made by an adult.

The Anabaptist movement was not homogenous. Three major

groups of Anabaptists were the Swiss-South Germans, the Moravian Hutterites, and the Dutch-Northwest German Mennonites. These groups, in this order, form a rough chronological account of Anabaptist developments. By the end of the sixteenth century, the groups had consolidated under the teachings of Menno Simons. The exception were the Hutterites, followers of Jakob Hutter (c. 1500–1536), who strongly advocated that Christian communities should hold all goods in common.

Today, several bodies are seen as descendants of continental Anabaptism: Mennonites, Amish, Hutterites, and Moravians. Baptist denominations share the emphasis of Anabaptism on believer's (adult) baptism in a "kinship" with Radical Reformation traditions.

Contemporary Anabaptists have maintained earlier emphases on Christian discipleship and the vital expression of the lordship of Christ in daily life. The church is the gathered community of disciples, and church discipline is an important mark of the Christian community. Anabaptists make a sharp distinction between church and world. Some, such as the Amish and the Hutterites, have maintained distinctive forms of dress from earlier periods that visibly mark their separation from the "world."

Anabaptists maintain the emphasis of Jesus on love and nonviolence. This translates into an advocacy of pacifism as the appropriate Christian means of existing in the world and resolving conflicts. Anabaptists stress freedom of religion and freedom of conscience as well as separation of church and state. They also emphasize the Holy Spirit as the means by which God's power and guidance is known in the community and in Christian lives.

95 What does the Reformation mean for us today?

From the perspective of five hundred years after the Protestant Reformation, we wonder why it is important and if it remains so?

Various answers are given to these questions. For some, the Reformation era is an interesting historical period, when people got "excited" about religion and set in motion ideas and practices that have "had their day" and now can safely be relegated to the dustbins of history.

But for others, the motivating issues of the Protestant Reformation continue to have significance. Biblical and theological insights from Reformers are found to be helpful in providing ongoing understandings for Christian faith. They provide guidance for Christians living in church contexts, and they nourish those who seek to be faithful followers of Jesus Christ in the world. Churches that emerged from the Reformation period maintain a central place in the Christian understanding and experience of millions of people of faith.

For these people, the Reformation has meaning today. Its teachings are a guide to ways of being Christian persons, even in environments and cultures vastly different from five hundred years ago. We can see a number of limitations of the Reformers, recognizing mistakes and blinders. But we can also gratefully build on their theological perceptions and visions as aids for our own Christian faith. Those in Reformation church traditions appropriate values of the traditions. They go on to develop the traditions through their own lives and witness as Christian persons. So the Reformation means a continuing deepening of faith.

A feature of the twentieth century was the growth of ecumenical relations among churches. Roman Catholic and Protestant churches have conducted theological dialogues. These have not led to obliterations of the past or a union of all churches into one, overall church body. But they have helped break down long-held stereotypes between Protestants and Roman Catholics and of Protestant churches with each other. They have spurred ecumenical relations among churches on local, congregational levels. These relations have helped Christians find commonality. They have shown that Christians who may disagree theologically—because of the Reformation, five centuries ago—can work together in common service to Jesus Christ who is "the head of the body, the church" (Col. 1:18) and the Christ who is "Lord of all" (Acts 10:36).

Beyond church contexts, the Protestant Reformation has clearly affected human history and particularly Western culture. A number of arenas in which the Reformation has been significant have been recognized. Not all historians agree on the implications of the Reformation in these areas, but several important dimensions can be mentioned.

Economics. A controversial book by the German sociologist Max Weber, *The Protestant Ethic and the Spirit of Capitalism* (English trans. 1930), proposed that Protestant ethics (especially in the Calvinist stream) encouraged people to work hard in the secular world, to carry out their Christian vocation, and to amass wealth that could then be invested. This, he argued, spurred the development of capitalism. It was further argued that some Protestants looked at the success of their ventures as a sign of their election or of being favored by God. Western capitalism flourished in strongly Protestant countries, such as Switzerland, England, and the United States. The Weber thesis has been criticized for a number of reasons, but it has been influential in arguing for an impact of Reformation thought and practice in influencing the emergence of Western economies.

Governance. Some scholars have argued for the influence of Protestant thought in fostering movements for religious liberty and freedom. Anabaptists resisted coercion in all matters of religion, seeking a strong separation of church and state. Luther's message of spiritual liberation was accompanied by the belief that the state should support the right to believe without interfering with individuals. Calvin stressed the right of the church to be free of state control. Calvin's thought also gave rise to views of the rights of resistance against governments that had transgressed their God-given limits or failed to carry out the will of God against tyrants. The Reformation promoted the growth of states and parliamentary-type governments with shared power and participation over traditional monarchical models. Western liberal democracies emerged.

Society. It has been noted that the Protestant Reformation brought wide changes to societal institutions in areas of constitutional law and order, criminal and family law, and laws of education and social welfare. Protestant emphases on education meant a move toward mass education through the establishment of schools, including schools for girls, as well as the founding of universities. Literacy was essential so that everyone could read the Bible. Relief for the poor and social care for those in need were prompted by Reformation concerns for love of neighbor. In some traditions these were ministries carried out on a widespread scale by church deacons, helping fuel a move toward institutionalized structures by governments to help those in need.

Some have also spoken of the "dark side" of the Reformation at various points insofar as it fueled anti-Semitism, persecution of witches, support of Nazism, and even the increase of suicides in some societies. All these are factors to be recognized. They stand in relation to the widespread positive Reformation influences on institutions that have mattered and continue to matter as they shape human societies, cultures, and religious lives.

For Further Reading

Bagchi, David, and David C. Steinmetz, eds. *The Cambridge Companion to Reformation Theology*. New York: Cambridge University Press, 2004.

Bell, James S., Jr., and Tracy Macon Sumner. *The Complete Idiot's Guide to the Reformation and Protestantism*. Indianapolis: Alpha Books, 2002.

Cameron, Euan. *The European Reformation*. New York: Oxford University Press, 1991.

Campbell, Ted A. *Christians Confessions: A Historical Introduction*. Louisville, KY: Westminster John Knox Press, 1996.

Collinson, Patrick. *The Elizabethan Puritan Movement*. Berkeley: University of California Press, 1967.

Dickens, A. G. *The English Reformation*. 2nd ed. University Park, PA: University of Pennsylvania Press, 1991.

Eire, Carlos M. N. *Reformations: The Early Modern World, 1450–1650*. New Haven, CT: Yale University Press, 2016.

Evans, G. R. *The Roots of the Reformation: Tradition, Emergence, and Rupture*. 2nd ed. Downers Grove, IL: InterVarsity Press, 2012.

George, Timothy. *Theology of the Reformers*. Nashville: Broadman Press, 1988.

Hillerbrand, Hans J. *The Division of Christendom: Christianity in the Sixteenth Century*. Louisville, KY: Westminster John Knox Press, 2007.

———. *The Encyclopedia of Protestantism*. 4 vols. New York: Routledge, 2004.

———. *Historical Dictionary of the Reformation and Counter-Reformation*. Historical Dictionaries of Religions, Philosophies, and Movements. No. 27. Lanham, MD: The Scarecrow Press, 2000.

———. *The Oxford Encyclopedia of the Reformation*. 4 vols. New York: Oxford University Press, 1996.

Holder, R. Ward. *Crisis and Renewal: The Era of the Reformations*. The Westminster History of Christian Thought. Louisville, KY: Westminster John Knox Press, 2009.

————. *The Westminster Handbook to Theologies of the Reformation*. The Westminster Handbooks to Christian Theology. Louisville, KY: Westminster John Knox Press, 2010.

Howard, Thomas Albert, and Mark A. Noll, eds. *Protestantism after 500 Years*. New York: Oxford University Press, 2016.

Lindberg, Carter. *The European Reformations*. Malden, MA: Blackwell Publishers, 1996.

MacCulloch, Diarmaid. *All Things Made New: The Reformation and Its Legacy*. New York: Oxford University Press, 2016.

————. *The Reformation: A History*. New York: Viking, 2003.

McKim, Donald K., ed. *Encyclopedia of the Reformed Faith*. Louisville, KY: Westminster/John Knox Press, 1992.

————. *Theological Turning Points: Major Issues in Christian Thought*. Atlanta: John Knox Press, 1988.

————. *The Westminster Dictionary of Theological Terms*. Rev. and exp. 2nd ed. Louisville, KY: Westminster John Knox Press, 2014.

O'Malley, John W. *Trent and All That*. Cambridge, MA: Harvard University Press, 2000.

Pettegree, Andrew. *Europe in the Sixteenth Century*. Blackwell History of Europe. Malden, MA: Blackwell Publishers, 2002.

Post-Reformation Digital Library. http://www.prdl.org.

Sunshine, Glenn S. *A Brief Introduction to the Reformation*. Louisville, KY: Westminster John Knox Press, 2017.

Tracy, James D. *Europe's Reformations, 1450–1650*. Critical Issues in History. Lanham, MD: Rowman & Littlefield Publishers, 1999.

Williams, George Huntston. *The Radical Reformation*. 3rd ed. Kirksville, MO: Sixteenth Century Journal Publishers, 1992.

CPSIA information can be obtained
at www.ICGtesting.com
Printed in the USA
FFOW03n0652220317
33693FF